Un

"Informative and entert...   e
the human-animal bon
has loved—a dog or cat

—Liz Palika, author of *The Ultimate Pet Food Guide*

"Dr. Shawn is a pet's best friend. *Unexpected Miracles* brings all attributes of prevention, holistic, and traditional medicine for pets to their owners."

—Dr. Jack L. Stephens, D.V.M., president and founder
of Pets Best Insurance

"Some pets make astounding recoveries if they can generate the body energy to repair. It is my hope that owners who read this book will seek integrative medicine for those pets who are entrusted to them."

—Dr. P. J. Broadfoot, D.V.M.

And for Dr. Shawn's previous titles

The Natural Vet's Guide to Preventing and Treating Cancer in Dogs

"A desperately needed bridge between the traditional and more natural cancer therapies . . . this book rates a 10+++, a win-win situation!"   —Carol Keppler, Intuitive Health

"A truly important book, vital to all dog owners. An ounce of prevention is worth a pound of cure, but with this book, you get a ton of each!"   —Jean Hofve, D.V.M.

Natural Health Bible for Dogs & Cats

"An excellent reference for veterinarians and pet owners alike."

—L. Phillips Brown, D.V.M., product manager
at Inter-Cal Nutraceuticals

"This bible is a 'new testament' that may help pet caregivers heal their sick pets."   —Alice Villalobos, D.V.M.

Unexpected Miracles

Hope and Holistic Healing
for Pets

Shawn Messonnier, D.V.M.

A Tom Doherty Associates Book

New York

UNEXPECTED MIRACLES
HOPE AND HOLISTIC HEALING FOR PETS

A Forge Book
Published by Tom Doherty Associates, LLC
175 Fifth Avenue
New York, NY 10010

www.tor-forge.com

Forge® is a registered trademark of Tom Doherty Associates, LLC.

ISBN-13: 978-0-7653-2089-6
ISBN-10: 0-7653-2089-4

First Edition: August 2009

Printed in the United States of America

0 9 8 7 6 5 4 3 2 1

Acknowledgments

In writing a book of this magnitude, there are always a number of people who have contributed to its successful completion. While I will name specific individuals, I apologize for leaving out anyone as it's easy to overlook someone.

First, to my editors, Claire Eddy and Kristin Sevick, and my agent, Marilyn Allen. All of you believed in me, my message of hope and healing, and this particular project, even when many others turned it down. Without your initial support, this book would never have become a reality.

I must also thank my staff. It's not easy being the boss, and sometimes my moodiness clouds the big picture. All of you do a great job helping me do a great job, and I am always indebted to your service and loyalty. Your efforts do not go unappreciated. Without your help, I would never be able to take time away from work in order to write. Thanks for not only holding down the fort but also keeping it well maintained in a holistic, caring way!

As always, my wife, Sandy, and daughter, Erica, put up with the absences and anxiety that often go along with writing a book. Thanks for your love and support. Everything I do is ultimately for you.

My faith in God has always been a source of inspiration. Everything I have and do is because of and hopefully for Him.

Thanks to all who have mentored me when I needed help, especially those who guided me as I was just learning about the wonderful field of integrative medicine.

Thanks to all those who provided various opportunities by opening doors for me to share my message with others. Thanks to my readers and radio-show listeners for your constant support and faith in my message.

A special thanks to Martha Stewart and all the good people at Martha Stewart Living Omnimedia and Sirius Satellite Radio, for supporting the message I bring to the readers of my column in *body+soul* magazine and listeners of my award-winning radio show.

Finally, the stories in this book are true, and they would never have occurred if not for my wonderful clients who choose health over illness. You refused to give up when others said all was hopeless. Your hope and passion, and the hard work it takes to conquer illness, inspire me and I know will inspire all those who read your stories. I hope I have not let you down and will continue to always strive to be the best so I can continue to help others experience their own "unexpected miracles."

Contents

Contents

Unexpected Miracles

Introduction

"Dr. Shawn, I'm so glad we found you. Nothing the other doctors have done have helped our pet. You're our last hope."

"I wish we had found you last year. We had to euthanize our dog because her doctor said nothing else could be done for her."

"No one else has given us any hope. We know the odds are against us. Even if alternative medicine doesn't work, we will try anything to save our beloved cat."

"I have no idea how any of these herbs or supplements work, but they are the only things that have stopped our pet's constant itching."

"Dr. Shawn, all of the specialists said that nothing could help our pet's cancer. Everyone else told us to go home and enjoy him for a few days until it was time to return for euthanasia. Thanks to all you've done, our pet is still alive two years after his original diagnosis."

These are just some of the many comments from grateful pet owners that I and my holistic colleagues around the world hear during a typical day at work. The pet owners who share these emotional comments with me are very thankful that I was able to help their pets.

I don't take all or even most of the credit, however. I only *facilitate healing* by having knowledge of many types of therapies. Ultimately, it is up to me to correctly diagnose the problem and to choose the best therapy; it is up to the owner to be able to implement the therapy (which is not always easy); and the pet's own unique ability to heal that determines the final outcome of any case.

Many years ago I searched for and found an alternative to the conventional medical training I received in veterinary school. It wasn't that I was unhappy as a conventional doctor, but rather that conventional medicine limited what I could do for my patients. By discovering the world of "alternative," "complementary," "integrative," or "holistic" care (all of these terms have been applied to what I do), I have been able to offer another solution to help pets for whom conventional medicine has not succeeded. While conventional medicine can help many pets with a number of diseases, especially acute illnesses or traumatic injuries, unfortunately, it is only one model of healing. When a conventional doctor or specialist can't help a patient, the prognosis is often "hopeless," and nothing more can be offered for the pet or caregiver. In reality, these doctors are speaking the truth as they know it, for there is "nothing more" that *they* can do. That doesn't mean that *someone* can't help the pet. The holistic doctor doesn't have to give up simply because one healing modality doesn't work.

No, holistic doctors like me have a variety of treatments from which we may choose. As a result, we see few truly "hopeless" cases, and are able to offer treatments to patients that have been given no hope by conventional veterinarians.

Not every pet can be saved, but hope can usually be given to all but the most moribund patients. Even when a cure cannot be offered, giving the family a few more days, weeks, months, or hopefully years with the pet is appreciated. When a pet fails to respond to all therapies, the humane practice of euthanasia can ease suffering and is better accepted by the family.

Since discovering all of these "alternative" treatments, I have seen fewer patients die from diseases that many doctors consider hopeless or incurable. I have seen many patients live longer, healthier lives by following a natural preventive program, as these pets rarely develop serious problems requiring life-long therapy with potentially toxic drugs. As a result, I enjoy coming to work more each day, knowing that I can offer something to these pets that may not be available to them anywhere else.

Some people may read this book and come to the opinion that I am "anticonventional medicine." Nothing could be further from the truth. I am a conventional doctor by training, and continue to learn as much as I can about conventional diagnostic and treatment modalities. Conventional medicine has its place in the treatment of both human and animal disorders. I use many conventional medical therapies as part of my overall treatment for my patients, but in a holistic fashion, using just enough medication to help the patient but not causing the side effects that commonly affect pets treated in a purely conventional manner. I appreciate the limits of conventional medicine and am realistic about what it can do for my patients. I'm not "antidrug," but rather "antidrugs for everything, everytime, everyplace no matter what," especially when there are better treatment options.

Holistic, alternative, complementary, and integrative are all terms associated with the type of healing presented throughout this book. Most doctors prefer holistic or integrative, as our approach focuses on the "whole" patient and integrates the most appropriate therapies needed to help heal the individual patient.

"Dr. Shawn, what do you do differently than other veterinarians?" is a question I get asked a lot from clients who are new to the field of holistic pet care. Each client has a different idea of what constitutes holistic, integrative care. Some think I use no conventional medicines or diagnostic testing, and are surprised when I recommend conventional medical therapies as part of their pets' overall treatment plan. Other clients come in for their pets' initial visit wanting a certain type of therapy, such as acupuncture or homeopathy. Still others have no real clue what to expect!

A few years ago I polled my colleagues in the American Holistic Veterinary Medical Association (AHVMA) to find out how they answered the question, "What do you do as a holistic doctor?"

One of my favorite answers came from a doctor who said that she moves energy. At first this answer seems quite strange and "out there," but the more we appreciate that, ultimately, every doctor's goal should be to help the patient heal itself, moving energy makes more sense. Even when I was trained only to offer conventional medicine I knew that I facilitated healing (another great answer to the question). Deep down I knew that I didn't actually heal my patients; they healed themselves if they were able to do so. If I chose the proper therapy, and if the pet was able to respond to the therapy, then the pet recovered. If the disease was too strong or the patient too weak, the disease would win.

As an integrative doctor, what I do now has not really changed all that much. I facilitate healing by moving the patient's own energy to heal itself. I also have many more therapies I can use than when I was only practicing conventional medicine. Most conventional medications are designed to make the patient feel better (cover up symptoms) or kill something (bacteria, fungi, viruses, or cancer). The goal of conventional medicine is not usually to heal the pet but rather to treat the disease. A more holistic approach appreciates that doctors don't really do anything except facilitate healing by correctly diagnosing the problem and then prescribing the best therapy for that patient.

Some skeptics who read this book might have some doubts. They may question my motives in writing the book. Simply, the pet lovers whose stories are shared here and I want pet owners everywhere to know that there is more to health care than conventional medicine alone. Conventional medicine has much to offer, and I use conventional diagnostic modalities and treatments every day. I am not opposed to these therapies, but I am opposed to closed mindedness. If our goal is to help the pet recover and stay well (stay healthy), does it really matter if the pet is treated with a combination of conventional medications, diet, herbs, homeopathy, nutrition, or any other alternative therapy?

Other skeptics who are opposed to an alternative approach to health care may feel that the stories I've shared in this book, some of them highlighting remarkable and at times even miraculous recoveries, are simply coincidental, or that the pets' recovery is simply the result of a placebo effect. The stories that I've selected for inclusion in this book are just a few of the thousands of similar accounts of pets who recovered from their illnesses by responding to a holistic approach to care after conventional medical practitioners had given up on them. No coincidences here, these are simply wonderful stories that show the power of an alternative approach to healing.

Many skeptics question whether a pet improves as a result of the placebo effect when treated with natural therapies. (In fairness, this question should also be asked about conventional therapies as well.) There are actually two ways that healing may occur when a patient is treated with any type of therapy. The first one is the aforementioned placebo effect, which is so commonly discussed when treating people: If a doctor prescribes a medication for someone with a hurt leg and tells his patient that he will improve in forty-eight hours, and then the patient improves, was it from the treatment or from the power of suggestion? Because our minds can often convince us that we feel better, it's difficult to know whether the response is from the therapy itself or from the mind telling the person that he is better.

Although this placebo effect often occurs in people, a pet

can't tell itself to feel better. If I give a pet a medication or supplement to make it stop itching, there is no way for me to tell the pet to stop itching. Either the treatment works or it doesn't. That's why this well-known placebo effect, which commonly occurs in people, cannot occur in pets. If the pet in this example stops itching, it must be the result of the treatment I chose.

The second type of placebo effect occurs in both people and pets. Simply put, many patients will improve no matter what treatment is chosen unless their condition is terminal. Holistic medical doctors and veterinarians can use the body's own healing ability to assist in wellness without resorting to powerful and expensive medications. It is a great thing—not a negative thing!— that the natural therapies we use can complement the body's own natural healing power. Just as you would choose the best therapies for your own body, it's important to do the same for your pet's body.

In the stories presented throughout this book, you will read how many of the pets I treated did not respond to conventional therapies prescribed by other conventional doctors. Their ultimate healing was neither coincidental nor the result of a placebo effect, but rather represents true healing as a result of the holistic therapies I prescribed for them.

My hope for you is that in reading this book, you will learn about the world of holistic healing. You will see that in many cases, simply because conventional medicine may not offer hope doesn't necessarily mean that another therapy can't help your pet. While there are never any guarantees, by exploring the world of holistic, integrative care, you will discover that there really can be "unexpected miracles" for cases once deemed hopeless.

1

How It All Started:

A Holistic Journey on the Road to Healing

Ask anyone who practices integrative medicine how it all started, and you'll get a variety of interesting answers.

Selecting a type of health care is very much a personal choice. For those of us who have chosen an integrative approach, defined as combining the best of conventional medicine with the best of natural therapies, the road began with a search for "something more" that conventional medicine was not able to offer.

Part of the journey for me involved a search to offer better care for my patients, and one fork in this road convinced me to share my healing discoveries with others through the books I've written. These books allow me to share with other doctors and pet owners around the world everything I have learned about natural pet care. As a result of these books, those of us who believe in the importance of integrative medicine are now changing the way we care for our pets.

Why did I begin my search for something more, and why did I feel the need to share this with readers around the globe? My search for holistic healing actually came about by accident. Like all conventional doctors, at one time I was very much anti-alternative medicine. I had heard of acupuncture and herbal therapies but really didn't know that much about them. We never had this information presented to us during our training in veterinary school, and it was never discussed in our professional journals or at continuing education meetings. Obviously, if there was any truth or validity to these alternative therapies, certainly they would have been taught to me and my classmates and presented regularly in the veterinary literature!

At the time I discovered alternative therapies and holistic healing, I wasn't even looking at the field of integrative medicine. Instead, I had become frustrated with the response, or rather lack of response, of all of my allergy cases to the treatments I was using at the time. The conventional approach to treating pets with allergies, the most common problem seen by many veterinarians, is the use of medications like corticosteroids (steroids) and antihistamines to control itching and inflammation, and antibiotics or antifungal drugs for pets with secondary infections. Some of the pets that don't do well with these drugs may improve with allergy testing and allergy shots (hyposensitization therapy). That's pretty much all conventional medicine can offer pets with allergies.

Antihistamines, as a class of drugs, don't work nearly as well in most pets as they do in people. Steroids, while very effective in reducing inflammation and itching in allergic pets, have many short-term and long-term side effects. While allergic pets treated with a steroid medication will stop itching almost immediately once the medication is given, they also usually start itching again once the steroid is stopped. Therefore, the owner and pet return shortly for more drugs, and the vicious cycle continues for the rest of the pet's life. Because steroids and antibiotics are used frequently in the treatment of allergic pets, their lives are ultimately shortened.

Many of my clients grew frustrated and impatient with this approach. They were coming in for regular visits, but their pets really weren't getting any better. The relief that the pets experienced with these conventional therapies was short-lived, necessitating frequent visits. The frequent visits added to the cost of pet care, and for some owners, the side effects their pets experienced with these conventional medications were unacceptable.

I shared the owners' frustrations with this approach. While I was temporarily making my patients feel better, I wasn't really helping them. In examining this approach, I felt that something was missing. There had to be something for my patients that would help them get better and stay better. I scoured the conventional literature and talked with a number of colleagues, including specialists in veterinary dermatology. Everyone told me that I was doing all that could be done for my patients. Still, I knew that there had to be something all of us were missing.

Then one day I found what I thought might be an introduction to the answer for which I was searching. I saw an ad in one of our veterinary journals for an enzyme product that purported to help pets with many problems, including allergies. At the same time, I read an article in another journal that talked about using fish oil to help allergic pets. I knew that fish oil could help pets with allergies, but I had never really seen any effect from using them. After reading this article, I discovered why fish oil had not worked well for my patients: the dose I was using, the one recommended in the conventional literature, was too low. By substantially increasing the dosage there was a chance for a better response.

Since nothing I had been taught seemed to help my allergic pets, I was open to trying anything to help them. Somehow at this time I discovered through my own trial and error that very frequent (even daily) bathing would help my allergic patients. This was contradictory to everything I had ever been taught. While these ideas were barely scratching the surface of integrative medicine, they did provide a starting point for me to begin trying to help my allergic patients.

I continued to learn about many of the various modalities of alternative medicine that I thought might help my patients, including nutrition and diet, supplements, herbs, acupuncture, and homeopathy. I began using these therapies on my allergic patients and started seeing much better and longer-lasting results than I had when I only used conventional medicine. The response I saw in my allergic patients encouraged me to learn more about integrative medicine and to holistically treat pets with other chronic disorders as well, including bowel disease, bladder disease, musculoskeletal problems, other skin conditions, immune problems, and even cancer.

As I was learning about this fascinating new world of integrative medicine, I had to admit something that was a bit uncomfortable. Even though I felt that I was a good doctor when I began my search, I was forced to admit that there simply had to be more than what I was already doing for my patients. While I had been trained to be a good diagnoser and treater of disease, I had to face the fact that I was not a good healer. My patients were feeling better, but the feeling was short-lived as their diseases returned and became chronic medical conditions. The end result was that my patients were not really healing, getting better and staying healthy, and many were dying at a younger age than I expected.

It would have been easy to continue what I had been doing since graduating from veterinary school. Although many of my patients never really healed from their disorders, they did feel better (if only for the time they were taking their medications.) I was making a good living and was doing the best I could with the therapies available to me.

I knew, however, that continuing down this path would not be the right thing to do. Simply taking money from a client and applying a Band-Aid solution to a more serious problem was not the road I wanted to continue to travel, and there was no turning back for me. I wanted healing for my patients, and I couldn't achieve that with the therapies I had been using. It was only when I admitted that I needed to become a *healer of pets* rather than a *treater of disease* that I could admit my own shortcomings and search for something better. This was not easy, because at the time I thought I was the best doctor that I could be and was doing all I could for my patients. I had to admit that I was wrong, which is never easy. I also had to accept that there were many pets I could have helped, had I known about integrative medicine at the time I treated them. While I had to accept the shortcomings in my education and training, it was not and still is not easy to know that I probably could have saved many of my patients if only someone had introduced me to this wonderful, natural world of healing. It wasn't really my fault since I had no clue about this alternative world of healing that I had begun to discover. This life-changing experience helped me realize that I shouldn't be too hard on my colleagues who have not yet been introduced to the wonders of integrative medicine. Nevertheless, I don't have such a soft heart for those who've been exposed to alternative therapies, yet continue to deny that these therapies have the ability to help their patients. Ignorance is one thing, but refusing to change your ways despite evidence that these therapies help your patients is at best neglectful and may one day even be considered malpractice.

Thankfully, my eyes were opened. Once I found this great new world of natural therapies, I started seeing positive results in most of my patients, many of whom I had not been able to help with conventional medicine alone. As a result, my practice motto became "Hope for the hopeless." I was now an ardent champion of every animal's chance at good health, and no longer did I have to tell a pet owner that I couldn't be of help, because now I had twice as many treatment options available.

Not wanting to be selfish with this newfound knowledge that gave hope and healing to many patients, I wanted to find a vehicle to share my excitement. That's when I started writing my books, newspaper column, and articles for various pet and veterinary journals. My own award-winning radio show soon followed, which meant I was able to share my message of healing with many more pet owners around the world who shared my desire to discover the secrets of health and longevity.

My five goals of healing for the patients you will read about in this book are as follows:

- **Prevent disease, as most owners prefer healthy rather than sick pets.**
- **Say *no* to drugs whenever possible, relying instead on natural therapies that tend to have few if any side effects when used properly, and often cost less than ongoing treatment with conventional therapies.**
- **Heal the pet rather than treat the disease, getting to the root of the problem and trying to find a long-term solution to keep the pet healthy.**
- **Reduce money spent on pet care, as no one wants to waste money on care a pet doesn't need.**
- **Finally and most important, offer hope for the hopeless, because our beloved pets rely on us and we should be committed to their health.**

These are goals that I could not possibly have developed when I practiced only conventional medicine. They also are the goals of the owners of the pets you will read about, ones I hope you will adopt as well as you begin your road to achieving health for your pets!

There you have it: my journey from the beginning to the present. It's taken a long time to go from believing exclusively in the value of only one system of medicine to embracing all healing modalities, but in the end, all of my patients benefit. Now you can share in this excitement as well as you discover the joys of healing you will find in these remarkable stories of pet owners who weren't willing to give up on their cherished companions.

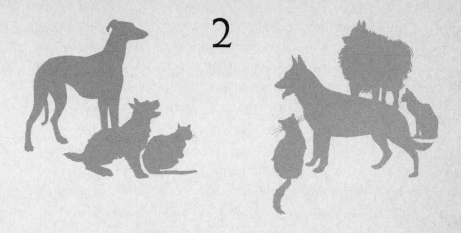

2

Beginning the Journey:

My First Case of Holistic Healing

Learning everything I possibly could about holistic healing for pets wasn't easy at first, as there was very little written information on the topic ten years ago. There was a lot of material on holistic healing in the human medical literature, however. While there are certainly important differences between people and pets, healing is still healing, and what I learned from the human medical literature was adaptable to my two- and four-legged patients.

I was also lucky that I found other veterinarians who were more than happy to share with me their passion for this wonderful field of integrative medicine. Several of my holistic colleagues in our international organization, the American Holistic Veterinary Medical Association, visited with me on the phone, answering questions and providing guidance. I met several colleagues at various veterinary meetings, picking their brains over lunch while they shared with me the healing modalities that worked best for specific problems. Manufacturers of various supplements, herbs, and homeopathics were likewise more than willing to share their knowledge and guidance as I set up my pharmacy for my integrative practice. The assistance of all of these experts was invaluable in helping me learn about this wonderful approach to patient care. I was happy to know that I would not be alone in my journey, but rather would have the support of many others who had blazed this trail before me, setting standards and taking risks that always come with trying something new despite a large amount of opposition from the conventional medical system. Studying anything new is certainly great and a lot of fun, but ultimately I wanted to apply this knowledge to help my patients. I was anxious and probably a bit impatient (an unfortunate character flaw) to get out of the books and into the examination room!

After studying diligently for several months, I knew the time would eventually come that I would actually have to see a real patient and try to put into action everything I thought I had learned. This was intimidating, and it reminded me of the anxious excitement I felt when I started my clinical rotations as a fourth-year veterinary student. Fortunately, I didn't have to look any further than my own staff to find my first holistic case.

Brit

About ten years ago, a nice young lady named Shelly was my receptionist who later moved up the medial-office ladder to become my first office manager. Not only did Shelly work for me for a while, and implement many of the current policies we still have in effect in our office, but her entire family had some involvement in my then growing practice. Her younger sister, Erin, was my first employee. Initially hired as a receptionist, she actually did anything and everything that was necessary in helping us become established in the local community in Plano, Texas. Her older sister, Tina, a registered nurse, filled in whenever Erin or Shelly needed the day off. Tina's training in the human medical field was an appreciated asset in dealing with clients and their pets. Shelly's mom, also an R.N., volunteered to step in on an emergency basis whenever we needed an extra hand. She once helped me force-feed a very ill blue and gold macaw, nursing it back to health and reuniting it with its grateful owner. Even the patriarch of the family, Shelly's dad, James, helped out fixing things around the hospital that seemed to break down. (I've always believed that veterinary school should have some sort of class on simple repairs, as every new practice owner invariably needs to spend a lot of money fixing things that break.)

Shelly had, at that time, a really sweet female boxer named Brittany (she called her "Brit"). I had been Brit's doctor since she was a puppy, spaying her and providing all of her general health care. She was a great dog and at the time the family's only pet. Everyone in Shelly's family took turns caring for Brit even though she was technically "Shelly's dog." By nature boxers are fun, happy, loving dogs, and I also developed a deep affection for Brit. It was hard not to forge a bond with a dog with large, sad, brown eyes that seemed to invite you to come over and pet her on the head. Of course, you always did so at your own risk as Brit, like most boxers, would be waiting to lick your face with her large, very wet, pink tongue.

Brit was a very healthy dog that had never been ill; she became my first case that I attempted to treat with integrative medicine. Cancer is quite common in boxers. As a matter of medical fact, they are the number-one breed to develop cancer, and anytime a sick boxer comes to my office, cancer is the first disease that comes to mind. Because of this, whenever I see boxer puppies I always make sure to spend some extra time with the owner to put in place a holistic pet program designed to reduce the chance of cancer.

Fortunately, Brit was not afflicted with cancer. Instead she had a condition I diagnosed as atopic dermatitis, also called atopy, which is commonly referred to as "allergies" by pet owners. It is common in many breeds of dogs, including West Highland white terriers (the number-one breed for this condition), Labrador and golden retrievers, and spaniels (especially cocker spaniels). While not commonly seen in boxers, Brit definitely was afflicted with allergies. Because she lived in Plano, Texas, one of the country's hot spots for poor air quality and many environmental allergens, the diagnosis was not too surprising. Skin conditions, especially atopic dermatitis, are among the most common medical problems I see in my practice.

Many owners mistakenly believe that the source of their pets' allergies is food. While food allergies can occur in pets, they are very rare. I've only seen one proven case of food-allergy dermatitis in more than twenty years of practice. Having said that, there is no question that eating poor-quality food does contribute to a whole host of medical problems for people and their pets. This is one of the reasons I always try to correct the diet of any pet that is being treated with integrative medicine, and why feeding the proper diet is the number-one step in my holistic healing program regardless of the pet's current health status. Without feeding the pet a proper diet, devoid of potentially harmful animal and plant by-products, chemical preservatives, and flavorings, my therapies won't achieve their maximum effectiveness. A proper diet is the foundation of every integrative therapy regardless of the disease afflicting the pet. While I always support owners who choose to prepare food for their pets at home, feeding them either cooked meals or a raw diet, the reality is that most owners find it more convenient to feed a prepared food. There are many different brands of prepared foods on the market, but I believe that most of them are worthless. They contain way too many chemicals and animal and plant by-products, which contribute to disease. Examples of some diets I currently recommend to my patients include Nature's Variety, Eagle Pack, Wysong, Innova, California Natural, Natural Balance, Blue, Wellness, and Trilogy.

That said, allergies in pets are usually due to environmental allergens. Most pets (and their allergic owners) have allergies to multiple allergens, including house dust mites, Bermuda grass, St. Augustine grass, fleas, cat dander, ragweed, and various other trees and plants. Allergy testing, done by veterinary dermatologists who inject small amounts of allergens within the skin and observe the pet's reactions, is necessary to diagnose exactly which allergens affect the pet. If the owner or doctor wants to treat the pet with frequent allergy shots, this testing must be done in order to know which allergens must be included in the shots.

In my practice, allergy testing is rarely needed, as my clients do not wish to pursue therapy with allergy shots and the integrative treatment of allergic dermatitis is the same regardless of which foreign proteins are bothering the pet. Since allergies are pretty easy to diagnose with a thorough medical history and a comprehensive physical examination, allergy testing is usually not needed in order to arrive at a diagnosis for most pets. Even though I had just completed learning the basics of integrative medicine, I must admit to being slightly intimidated at facing this first case. It's one thing to read about something, but it's totally different when you have to try to apply this new knowledge to an actual clinical case. And not to brag, but veterinary employees really look up to their bosses. While I don't quite walk on water in the eyes of my employees, I at least occasionally part the seas! I really wanted to use my new therapies to successfully treat Brit's allergies.

Regardless of the approach, conventional or integrative, I always start with a good history and physical examination to assist in making the diagnosis. (In the case of pets with allergies, usually the diagnosis is made just from these two steps.) Often other problems related to the allergies, such as an ear or skin infection, will also be discovered. Additionally, many times when I examine a pet for a specific problem, I will find something totally unrelated such as heart disease or dental disease. *Since the integrative approach focuses on the patient and not the disease*, it's really important to identify other problems that may coexist with the owner's original complaint. Sometimes, these additional problems may be even more important or detrimental to the pet's health than the original complaint and must be addressed as well.

Fortunately, Brit had no other problems that I discovered or that Shelly mentioned during the initial visit.

Shelly initiated the conversation by telling me that Brit, who was not normally an itchy dog, started itching several weeks prior to this visit. Over the past few days, the intensity of her itching had increased a lot.

During my examination, I noticed that Brit's skin looked pretty normal, except for a few areas of irritation that were reddened and bore marks of her scratching her itchy skin. It's not unusual for itchy pets to have essentially normal skin. One of the ways I determine that the cause of itching is due to allergies is the appearance of "normal skin in an itchy dog." Occasionally, I'll actually see skin lesions on an allergic pet, such as pustules (pimples), papules (tiny red bumps), or scabs or crusts, which represent a secondary infection with bacteria or yeasts. Since allergic skin is not normal, secondary infections occur more easily in allergic pets. I would estimate that about 50 percent of the allergic pets I see have a secondary infection. These infections by themselves can be very itchy, and they must be treated correctly in order to reduce the pet's level of itching. If the infections are not properly diagnosed and treated, the pet will never get better.

A common cause of repeated and chronic skin infections is

allergic dermatitis. (Food sensitivity and thyroid disease also predispose a pet to skin infections.) Unless the underlying allergies or other problems are discovered, the pet will continue to suffer from chronic infections.

Since Brit didn't have any obvious skin infections at this first visit, my only concern was to address her allergies. That sounds simple enough, but this was over ten years ago and I had just started learning about holistic care! I had a lot of thoughts but still wasn't sure that I had the ability to actually help a real patient.

Complicating matters at the time was a simple fact of a holistic, integrative approach to medicine: *Each patient is an individual and is to be treated as such.* I've learned since this first case that while there are guidelines in treatment, no two cases are exactly alike, and there is often no one way to deal with a certain medical problem. This is why it's impossible for me to accurately answer a question owners often pose to me, "How would you treat my pet with (name of the disease)?" I have no idea how I would treat such a pet until I see the pet and thoroughly review the case!

The holistic approach, in my opinion, is often more art than science (although we have a lot of science to back up our chosen therapies). This means that the holistic doctor must take time to properly evaluate each case. The pet owner is a partner in the diagnosis, treatment, and healing of the pet. Ultimately our goal is to heal the pet, rather than treat a disease (a very different approach than the one I had learned in my conventional medical career). Healing is a lifelong process, whereas simply helping the pet feel better and treating a disease lasts only a short period of time.

With all of these thoughts swimming around in my head, I somewhat timidly decided to offer Shelly several therapies that might offer Brit some help. I was very grateful that Shelly appreciated my initial timidity and hesitation, just as I was grateful that she was open to trying whatever would make Brit feel better in the short term and also heal in the long term. I chose to treat Brit with several natural therapies that I had just learned about. First, I had recently learned a few acupuncture techniques and was eager to try them. I chose to treat Brit by gently inserting acupuncture needles into various points that have been shown to help with skin diseases and to regulate the immune system.

Acupuncture is without a doubt one of the most field-tested techniques available in complementary medicine, having been around for thousands of years. There are numerous acupuncture points in the body that lie over free nerve endings wrapped in connective tissue or within the walls of blood vessels. While the exact mechanisms by which acupuncture achieves its healing effects is still debated, we do know that through some neurohormonal process, healing is stimulated and pain and inflammation are relieved.

Like all pet owners, Shelly was worried that acupuncture would be painful and hurt her pet. Usually acupuncture is not painful. As I explained to her, occasionally a pet will experience some sensation as the needle passes through the skin. Once in place, most animals will relax, and some may become sleepy. Fractious animals (especially cats and nervous dogs) may require mild sedation for treatment. I've had acupuncture done to myself, and for the most part it was not uncomfortable. (I actually closed my eyes and relaxed during most of my treatment sessions.)

While all therapies, including natural therapies, have side effects, those associated with natural therapies are usually very rare and not serious when compared with the side effects that commonly occur with many conventional medications. Like other holistic treatments, side effects from acupuncture are rare. Accidental puncture of an underlying vital organ can occur; this usually happens if the wrong size needle is chosen and then placed (the needles come in various sizes, and the correct length of needle must be chosen that corresponds to the size of the pet and the area to be treated) in an area where there is minimal soft tissue that covers the underlying organs (such as the abdomen). Infection can occur at the site of needle insertion; needles should not be placed in areas where the skin is infected or inflamed. Occasionally, the needle can break (due to patient movement or incorrect needle placement and removal) and surgery may be needed to remove it. Some pets require sedation in order to allow insertion of the acupuncture needles. Finally, in some patients, clinical signs may worsen for a few days before they improve. (This is not unusual in pets treated with complementary therapies, as the body is going through the healing process; in fairness, some animals treated with conventional medications also get worse before the medication kicks in and the pet begins to show signs of improvement.) Shelly appreciated my frank discussion of acupuncture with her, and was relieved to see that Brit did not mind her acupuncture treatment at all.

As is true with the goal of healing that all holistic doctors have for their patients, there is no one therapy that is best for each case. In fact, multiple therapies are usually chosen to heal the patient. Their use has an additive effect that better and more quickly promotes healing. In addition to Brit's acupuncture treatments, I prescribed the following therapies to help her heal from her recent allergy attack.

Fatty acids (fish oil) were one of the first "natural" therapies to be embraced by conventional doctors. Their original application was in the treatment of skin disease, specifically allergic dermatitis. Now we know that fatty acids have many other applications in human and veterinary medicine, including the treatment of heart disease, hypertension, cancer, kidney disease, arthritis, depression, and any condition that may have an inflammatory component. Fatty acids, specifically the omega-3 fatty acids EPA and DHA found in the oils of cold-water fish, have significant anti-inflammatory activity. EPA and DHA are actually incorporated into the cell membranes, resulting in less inflammation whenever allergens are present and cause cell damage. Therefore, it was an easy decision to choose fish oil along with Brit's acupuncture regimen. I prescribed a high dose of fish oil for her, approximately 1,000 mg of EPA and DHA, which is much higher than the dose on the label of fish-oil products. The label dose is really more of a maintenance dose for healthy coats. To get the medical benefits of fish oil needed to prevent or treat problems, doses several times those listed on the label are typically needed.

While I prescribed a high-quality dog product for Brit, I often have owners ask if it's okay to use a "people" product for their pets. In general the answer is yes, if the following precautions are taken. The form of the supplement must be easy to administer to the pet. (Pet products are often flavored to make administration easy for the owner.) The dosage of the product must be correct. (Most people products are not formulated in the correct dose for pets, which surprisingly is often higher than that needed for people.) A quality manufacturer must be selected to ensure safety, efficacy, potency, and purity of the product. Because few "people" supplements fulfill these requirements, I prefer pet products for my patients. For fatty-acid supplementation, I typically prescribe a pet supplement called Ultra EFA by Rx Vitamins *for* Pets for my patients, as I did for Brit.

Because Shelly worked for me, she knew I only prescribed high-quality supplements for pets. Too often I see pet owners purchasing products off the Internet, or at the local health or pet store. Very often they purchase these supplements without a doctor's advice and with no knowledge of what they are actually buying for their pets. Maybe they see a fancy ad for the product, or take the well-intentioned advice from a store clerk who is trying to help the owner pick the best product. There is usually little harm in purchasing something such as a daily health supplement designed to maintain health without the advice of a veterinarian, but it's critically important that owners follow the advice of a veterinarian when choosing supplements to help heal a pet with a disease. While supplements are safe, they can and do make pets sick, interacting poorly with other supplements or conventional prescription medications. For safety's sake, it's always best to check with your veterinarian before using any supplement for your pet.

While fish oil is a great supplement to help pets with allergies, it is not the only supplement I use. In trying to formulate a

plan that would have the greatest chance of successfully helping Brit, I also picked a potent pet antioxidant called Proanthozone by Animal Health Options (I also like Rx Essentials by Rx
Vitamins *for* Pets, Super-Ox by Nutri-West, and Cell Advance
by Vetri-Science). Oxidation occurs as a result of cell damage,
and the clinical signs seen in pets with allergic dermatitis definitely occur as the result of significant cell damage.

Additionally, various Western and Chinese herbs are very
helpful in healing allergic pets. Herbs are made from parts of
plants that have shown medicinal properties. Like the conventional medications antihistamines and corticosteroids, often
prescribed for pets with allergies, herbs act as powerful natural
medicines. In Brit's case, I chose a product called Silerex by Evergreen Herbs which has steroid-like and antihistamine-like effects, reducing inflammation and itching, and helping the skin
to heal.

Even though I regularly use homeopathy in the care of my patients, at the time I first saw Brit I had not yet really grasped this
healing modality. In this interesting alternative therapy, diluted
remedies are given to the pet to stimulate healing by increasing
the pet's own energy. Now I use many homeopathic remedies
made by the Heel company in treating skin as well as other problems, and see even greater results in my patients. I also now prescribe a product called Vim & Vigor by Pet-Togethers for my
itchy patients. It was not available at the time I treated Brit, but
fortunately pet owners can now use this wonderful, balanced
product that has been lifesaving for many of my allergic patients.

Finally, a very important part of healing Brit's skin involved topical therapy. In her case, it meant frequent bathing with an aloe vera and colloidal oatmeal shampoo, followed by a conditioner containing the same anti-itching ingredients. I'm not sure who started the urban legend that you shouldn't bathe pets often, but in my opinion the *most* important part of treating skin diseases involves cleaning the skin frequently.

Frequent bathing must be done in order to accomplish several goals: It cleanses the skin of any bacteria and yeast. It also reduces inflammation and itching. For Brit, frequent bathing literally removed the allergens landing on her skin before she could absorb them into her body and experience an allergy attack. The more frequently pets like Brit are bathed, the less often they will require steroids or other drugs to control their itching and inflammation, and the sooner they will heal from their skin diseases. Many good products are available from veterinarians, including those made by Vet Solutions, Virbac, DVM Resources, and my own line of USDA certified organic shampoos, Dr. Shawn's Pet Organics.

How frequently should pets with skin diseases be bathed? The easy answer is that they cannot be bathed too often *if* the proper shampoo is used. Despite what you may have heard, regular bathing of dogs and cats will *not* dry out their skin, anymore than your own regular bathing dries out your skin. And if the skin does become a bit dry, it's easy to treat this by following the bath with a conditioning rinse or an application of a humectant or a moisturizer.

Think of it this way: Let's suppose you have dandruff, a really common skin problem that affects many of us from time to time. If you read the label on the bottle of shampoo, it's recommended to use the product at least one to two times daily until the dandruff is well controlled. The same advice holds true for pets with skin disease.

While it is important to frequently bathe pets with skin disease, it's not always the easiest task for owners to accomplish, especially if your pet does not like being bathed. If possible, it would be best to start bathing your pet when it is a puppy or kitten to acclimate it to this procedure. If your pet is not used to being bathed, especially when dealing with a cat, the procedure must be done gradually in order to produce the least amount of trauma for your pet. Placing the pet into a bathtub that already contains a small amount of water and gently pouring the water with a cup over the pet eliminates the trauma that can be associated with the sound of running water. Alternatively, using a shower massage head to gently put the water directly onto the pet's skin can also be effective, and it is a technique I use at my office when bathing pets.

Finally, your pet may need some sort of natural calming therapy or even a conventional sedative if it finds the bathing procedure to be overly traumatic. And even though frequent bathing is important, keep in mind that any bathing is helpful. The more frequently your pet can be bathed, the less conventional medication you will need to use to heal its skin, and the quicker your pet will be healed.

In Brit's case, I had Shelly bathe her daily for one week, weaning her down to every two to three days as she improved. For maintenance, Shelly bathed her several times per week. Granted, it was easy to bathe Brit frequently since Shelly used the elevated bathtub at our hospital and Brit, always a cooperative patient, loved being bathed. Still, I've found that most pet owners can adapt and bathe their pets at least a few times a week. Like Shelly, pet owners who can frequently bathe their pets usually find that the skin heals more quickly and that fewer conventional medications are needed.

Feeding the proper diet must form the foundation of any holistic healing plan. While I was not as attuned to its importance ten years ago, when I first began my holistic career, I knew that Brit needed to eat wholesome food with as few by-products and additives as possible. These are commonly put into processed foods, for people as well as pets, and they only contribute to ill health, inflammation, and oxidation. As Brit had enough inflammation and oxidation already, choosing a healthy diet made sense. The only problem was that ten years ago we had few high-quality natural diets available. Now there are many manufacturers that make great holistic diets, and many of my clients also choose to prepare a fresh raw or cooked diet at home. Therefore, Shelly and I did the best we could for Brit, choosing one of the few natural diets on the market at the time that seemed to be the most healthful for her.

Finally—and I cannot stress this enough—*it's an accepted medical fact that no pet needs vaccines every year!* Current research shows that our pet vaccines can induce long-lasting immunity, in some cases for many years after the pet has been vaccinated. Back when I first treated Brit, this medical fact was suspected but not yet proven or accepted by the conventional medical establishment. (Even many holistic veterinarians didn't know then the best recommendation for immunization.) Using what little knowledge I had of immunity, vaccination, and health at that time, Shelly and I made the decision not to further vaccinate Brit unless her allergies were well controlled by our holistic treatment plan. Continuing to give her unnecessary vaccinations would not only be a waste of time and money but also could make her allergies worse. Today I see many pets whose allergies have been well controlled with our integrative approach to treatment. Often an owner will return to her regular veterinarian for maintenance care and, not following the advice I gave at our initial visit, will have the pet vaccinated again. Within a few days or weeks following the vaccinations the pet is once again itching, and we have to start our therapy all over again. This causes considerable discomfort to the pet and an unnecessary medical bill for the owner.

I now take a different approach to immunization in my holistic practice. I do a blood test called an antibody titer test that measures each pet's antibody levels to specific diseases such as parvovirus or distemper. If these titer levels are low, *and* if the pet is healthy *and* not too old, I may vaccinate based upon titer testing. Since I began focusing on health rather than disease, proper diet and nutritional status, and reducing vaccinations and other unnecessary medications (like regular flea and tick medications that most pets do not need), I have seen my patients stay healthier longer and rarely become ill.

While many conventional veterinarians continue to vaccinate all their patients on a regular basis (every six to twelve months), even those with serious or chronic diseases, there is no need to do so. Pets can form long-lasting immunity from currently available vaccinations. For greater discussion of this, see Appendix A, "Vaccination Concerns."

I would like to say that Brit was treated successfully without the use of conventional medications, but that was not to be. As I mentioned, Brit was my first integrative case, and I did need to use some medications to help her feel better quickly. I had hoped that my use of alternative therapies would be enough to help Brit heal, and was somewhat discouraged that she still needed some conventional medications to feel better. I have since learned, however, that many of my patients might need a small amount of various conventional medications at the start of my therapy to help them feel better quickly, while the alternative treatments I use will produce longer-lasting results and cause the ultimate healing that the owners and I seek for the pet.

Prednisone is a steroid that immediately relieves itching, redness, and inflammation in pets with allergies. Many pet owners are reluctant to use steroids due to a whole host of long-term side effects like osteoporosis, diabetes, increased infections, and weight gain. Nevertheless, using steroids on a short-term, low-dose, as-needed basis is very safe and very effective. Shelly, too, was reluctant to put her pet on such a potent medication, but I talked her into using prednisone orally for just a few days. As soon as Brit stopped itching and the natural therapies began working, Shelly stopped giving her the prednisone on a regular basis as it was no longer needed.

This first attempt at using integrative medicine proved to be a success for both Brit and me. As Brit improved, we decreased the frequency of her acupuncture therapies to on an as-needed basis. Within only two months we were actually able to stop acupuncture altogether, and only used it a few times a year when Brit's allergies flared up to jump-start her immune system and hasten her healing.

Shelly rarely needed to continue using steroids or other medications on a regular basis because the natural supplements were what really helped heal Brit. When her skin flared up, which occurred only a few times each year, Shelly would use a low dose of prednisone for just a few days and would double up on the supplements.

Certainly success with my first case did not prove that a holistic approach to helping pets would always work. Still, had this pet not improved it would have been very tempting to become frustrated and give up. Fortunately, the success I had with Brit provided the impetus to continue learning and moving forward. Although I originally learned about natural therapies to help my allergic patients, little did I know that I would soon get to test the holistic approach on another memorable case with a much more serious problem.

3

One Disease, Four Outcomes

Shasta

Shortly after my initial success healing Brittany's allergies, I had the opportunity to see another favorite client and pet, Linda and her big furry dog, Shasta, a middle-aged female dog, a combination of chow and golden retriever, who had come to our office for her annual September checkup. (Keep in mind that we do this checkup twice yearly on pets five years of age and older in an attempt to diagnose serious diseases that occur more commonly in older pets *before* the pet actually becomes ill with a disease.)

While I always enjoyed seeing Shasta and Linda, Shasta was

always cautious and protective of her owner during her annual visits. No doubt the chow in Shasta made her personality such that she wasn't outwardly friendly and always required muzzling to allow the staff and me to properly handle her.

At the time of this visit, I still practiced a lot of conventional medicine. I didn't really appreciate the importance of vaccine titer testing at the time as it was not being done regularly. These tests, which we use in lieu of vaccines, simply let me know if and when a pet requires immunizations. Titer testing has revealed to me that most pets rarely need immunizations, and certainly not on an annual basis. When I saw Shasta many years ago, annual vaccinations were still recommended by all of the conventional veterinary experts (who now recommend vaccinating no more than every three years). As a result, during this visit we planned to do our normal protocol of vaccines for Shasta if I didn't discover any health problems during the visit. Shasta had always been a very healthy patient, and to date had not had any major medical problems other than a mild flea infestation a few summers prior to this visit.

There are several parts to a pet's annual visit. The first part involves questioning the pet owner about any particular concerns that she may have regarding her pet. For example, has the pet's appetite decreased or increased since her last visit? What is the pet's water consumption like? Any change in the pet's behavior? What about changes in bowel movements and urinary habits? Has the pet experienced any coughing or vomiting, difficulty walking, getting up and down, or playing? Very often the answers to these questions will elucidate an underlying problem that the owner might forget to mention during the annual visit. The best time to diagnose a problem is when the pet still acts healthy, so it's important for me to spend time questioning the owner to make sure there aren't any obvious problems the owner or other family members have observed. In Shasta's case, Linda reported no abnormalities.

The second part of our annual visit involves the full physical examination, during which I check as many organ systems as possible. The physical actually begins the minute the pet enters our hospital. Sometimes the receptionist will notice something when the pet walks in, or my assistant will notice a problem as she's weighing the pet and putting it into the examination room. Even when I'm talking with the owner for a few minutes at the start of the visit, obtaining the history, I'm always carefully observing the pet's behavior. Is the breathing too rapid? How do the pet's skin, hair, and eyes appear? Does it exhibit any stiffness or signs of pain when moving around the room? I'm constantly scanning the pet for even the slightest, most subtle difference from the normal.

The hands-on part of the examination begins as I lift the pet from the floor onto the examination table. I want to make sure the pet is comfortable being handled and lifted, and doesn't show any signs of pain or discomfort. In Shasta's case, she did not offer any resistance to being picked up, although it did appear as if her abdomen was a bit tense.

After putting Shasta on the examination table, I ran my hands up and down her body. I wanted to make sure that I could easily feel her ribs and spine, which would indicate adequate body muscling and fat without being overweight (a very common problem in pets *and* their owners!) or being overly thin. This hands-on feeling of the pet's skeleton and flesh gives me an idea of its body composition index, a better indication of its fat-to-muscle ratio than from simply weighing it. I also carefully note if there are any tumors or warts that require my attention. In Shasta's case, her weight and body composition were normal and had not changed from her last visit, and no tumors or warts were noted.

I then proceeded with the rest of Shasta's examination. I carefully looked into her ears for signs of infection or inflammation. I noticed her eyes were clear and did not exhibit abnormal drainage. I noted a small amount of dental tartar when doing an examination of her oral cavity, indicating periodontal disease. This is the most common infectious disease seen in pets, affecting almost 100 percent of dogs and cats three years of age and older. We had cleaned Shasta's teeth the prior year, and I mentioned to Linda we would need to do this again shortly if no other problems were discovered.

I then listened to Shasta's heart and lungs with my stethoscope, carefully searching for any abnormal sounds, which can indicate heart disease or bronchitis, also common in older dogs. Fortunately, her heart and lungs sounded normal.

I keep the pet comfortable and make the experience as pleasant and stress free as possible by being very subtle during most of the visit, examining the pet as I'm stroking her and talking with the owner. In many instances I'm finished with the exam before the pet or owner knows what I've done. While this makes the visit very easy for the pet, and is likely a major reason why most pets actually enjoy their visits at our hospital, I've had several new first-time clients who were not even aware that the exam was completed during our conversation. This can cause problems when owners leave the office at the end of the visit and ask the staff whether or not their pets are going to be examined that day! A careful explanation of my gentle, holistic examining technique usually puts them at peace, and most appreciate the fact that their pets don't mind coming to our office for their checkups.

Finally I completed Shasta's examination by carefully palpating (feeling) her abdomen and lymph nodes, which were normal in size and feel, but I noticed her abdomen was enlarged. It was also a bit tense and difficult to palpate. Nevertheless, what I could palpate was a large, round mass in the center of her belly. This was definitely not normal, and I suspected it was a sign of a serious disease.

Dogs with abdominal masses, especially large breeds five years of age and older, don't have many easily treatable diseases that produce these masses. The main possibilities are tumors of the liver or spleen, and in most cases these are highly malignant and have been present for some time when finally diagnosed.

All of us fear getting the diagnosis of cancer for ourselves or a loved one. It's no different when that loved one is a four-legged member of your family. As a veterinarian who deals with cancer on a daily basis, I appreciate that it's always difficult to break the news to an owner that a pet may have cancer, especially when the pet is not ill and was brought to the office for a totally different reason. Consequenty, when an office visit was supposed to be for an annual checkup for an apparently normal pet, the news of possible cancer must be delivered gently and delicately.

So it was that I needed to tell Linda that her special companion might have an abdominal tumor that could be malignant. Because tumors may grow if vaccines are administered, I told Linda that we should not do any shots for Shasta that day. I didn't overwhelm her with too much information that she would not be able to fully process, as she had not planned for this diagnosis at today's visit. At times like this I prefer to be as positive as possible while still relating to owners that we need to move forward quickly in order to do the best for their pet. It's a delicate balancing act, and I know that all owners end up leaving my office fearing the worst. Still, I think it's good to prepare them for something bad while still trying to be as positive as possible until we have the full picture.

The third and final part of our annual checkup involves laboratory testing. A great history provided by an insightful, caring owner, and a thorough physical examination are very important, but some information can only be obtained by performing laboratory testing to look inside the pet's body. While I would normally draw blood on Shasta as part of her annual health checkup, it was even more critical that I do this upon finding her abdominal mass during the physical examination. I drew blood for diagnostic testing while she patiently offered her left front leg, and then scheduled Shasta for radiographs the following day.

Her blood testing revealed an increased level of her liver enzymes, and the abdominal radiographs showed an enlarged liver. At this point all of the testing pointed to the probability of liver cancer. I gently broke the news to Linda, who was not too surprised as I had prepared her with my initial suspicions during her visit the preceding day. I started Shasta on some supplements to help support her diseased liver, and I referred Linda to our local oncologist for consultation about the possibility of treatment (chemotherapy or surgery) to help Shasta.

Deep down I knew that if my suspicions of liver cancer proved correct after the visit to our local specialist, there would not be much that the specialist could do for Shasta. Unless diagnosed very early in the course of the disease (which rarely happens since most pets with liver cancer don't act sick until the end stages of the disease), liver cancer is usually nontreatable and considered hopeless by practitioners of conventional medicine.

Of course, my suspicions were right. The local oncologist reviewed everything I had done and also performed an abdominal ultrasound examination to get a better look at the liver mass. She also performed an aspirate of the mass and looked at the cells under a microscope. There was no doubt in her mind that Shasta did in fact have liver cancer, a specific kind called hepatic adenocarcinoma.

This diagnosis is usually a death sentence for the pet, as there are no really effective chemotherapy drugs to help fight this cancer. And unless the tumor is confined to only one lobe of the liver, it can't be removed surgically. The bad news for Shasta was that the cancer involved her entire liver, meaning there were no conventional therapies that could offer Linda or Shasta any hope of recovery, much less a cure.

Linda and I discussed the findings of the specialist and the hopeless prognosis given Shasta. She was heartbroken at the unexpected diagnosis of cancer, and asked me if there was anything at all that I could offer Shasta. It was early September, and her oldest son, Jason, a college sophomore studying accounting, was currently away at school in another state and would not be home until the Christmas holidays. Because Shasta was really his dog and a companion since he was a young boy, Linda was willing to try anything to keep Shasta alive until he could see her one last time.

I reiterated to Linda that there was nothing conventional medicine could offer to help Shasta remain alive even for a few months. The usual prognosis for advanced hepatic adenocarcinoma is a few weeks—usually two to three from the time of the diagnosis—due to its advanced and aggressive nature by the time of diagnosis. Euthanasia usually follows, as the pet's condition rapidly declines.

At this time, early in my holistic career, I was reading everything I could possibly find on using natural therapies to help pets. Coincidentally, I had just read an article in my journal from the AHVMA about using herbs to treat liver cancer in rats. While rats and dogs are certainly not the same creatures, from a holistic/Eastern/Chinese approach, that doesn't really matter. Disease is viewed the same regardless of the species or even the cause. Ultimately the herbs mentioned in the short article were designed to slow down the growth of cancer and help the liver heal as much as possible for as long a period of time as possible.

I told Linda that I was pretty new at this holistic stuff, but wanted to offer her and Shasta some hope. As a conventional doctor, I knew there was nothing I or anyone else in that field of medicine could do for them. As a holistic doctor, I was willing to try if she was also willing. In essence, I explained, Shasta would be a guinea pig, my first cancer patient on whom I would try this holistic treatment. Linda was desperate for anything that might give her just a bit more time with Shasta. While I knew she was hoping for several months of life so that her son would be able to make it home to spend some time with Shasta, I told her I would do my best. Deep down, I didn't think I could give Shasta that long to live.

Approximately two weeks had passed since my original diagnosis, and Shasta was now starting to show signs of her progressive cancer. She had lost about five pounds, her spine was becoming prominent, indicating muscle wasting, and her appetite had decreased. I knew that in addition to any of the natural therapies I wanted to use, I would also have to combine some conventional medications to help Shasta increase her food intake and feel better. I therefore put together a truly integrative program, combining conventional medications plus whatever supplements I had at my disposal.

Since Shasta's appetite had decreased, I prescribed a medication called oxazepam for her. This drug, similar in chemical structure to diazepam, or Valium, is typically considered a sedative. However, when administered in a lower dosage than is typically used for sedation, it can increase appetite in some pets. I've used it successfully in many patients on a short-term basis when needed to jump-start appetite. I've never seen any side effects in my patients from this drug, and hoped that just a few days' worth of the medication would be all I needed to get Shasta eating more again.

I also wanted Linda to try to encourage Shasta to eat whatever she wanted. We know that cancer cells thrive on diets high in carbohydrates and low in fatty acids and protein—the typical dog food most dogs are fed! The recommended diet for cancer patients is high in protein, high in fatty acids (fish oils), and low in the starchy carbs found in cereal grains. The *best* diet for any cancer patient, however, is the one that the pet will eat! Therefore, for my cancer patients who are not eating well, I encourage the owners to feed the pets anything they will eat. I also prescribe a liquid diet called CliniCare that is very useful in boosting the pet's appetite. It can be fed as the sole diet or to add more calories to an undernourished pet. Since Shasta's cancer was taking in nutrients that she needed to fight the cancer, I had Linda add CliniCare as needed to Shasta's daily diet.

At this same time, I had the opportunity to frequently consult with the oncologist who saw Shasta during her referral, on a variety of other interesting cases that we were both treating. The oncologist, one of the few in our area who is very open to integrative medicine, had told me about using a drug called piroxicam in many of her cancer patients. Piroxicam is a nonsteroidal anti-inflammatory medication (NSAID) often used to relieve pain and inflammation in people. In dogs, it is commonly prescribed for cancer patients in an attempt to reduce the amount of cancer in the body. Ten years have passed since I treated Shasta, and doctors now know much more about how NSAIDs might help relieve cancer in pets. At the time I was treating Shasta, all we knew was that a very small number of pets with cancer who were prescribed piroxicam lived longer or were cured, even of incurable cancers. Since we had nothing to lose, I wanted to try this conventional drug as part of my therapy to try to help Shasta live longer with her incurable cancer. Even though piroxicam can have some serious side effects typical of all NSAIDs (most commonly ulcers of the gastrointestinal system, which thankfully I've never seen in my cancer patients), it was worth trying, as Shasta had basically been given a death sentence due to the aggressive nature of her liver cancer.

I also prescribed several supplements to try to detoxify Shasta and support her liver. The supplements I chose were Liver DTX by Evergreen Herbs, a Chinese herbal remedy that contained the same herbs that I had read about in my veterinary journal that were very effective in helping rats with liver cancer. Immuno Support and Hepato Support by Rx Vitamins *for* Pets were also chosen to help Shasta fight her liver cancer. Immuno Support is a potent formula designed to help boost a pet's immune system. It's a great supplement whenever an immune system needs help, and cancer patients certainly do need a strengthened immune system. If their systems were functioning properly, these patients would never have developed cancer. Rx Vitamins *for* Pets now has an even better immune-supporting supplement called ONCO Support. Years in the making, it is one of the best supplements for pets with cancer.

The first two weeks of therapy were tough for Linda and Shasta. Shasta's appetite was down and her attitude was slightly depressed. Still, Linda hung in there and was able to get Shasta to eat some of her favorite foods on her own, supplementing her with the liquid CliniCare I prescribed. The appetite-stimulating oxazepam took a few days to work, but when it did Shasta regained her appetite. As her nutritional status improved, and her liver inflammation decreased as a result of the supplements Linda was administering to her, Shasta's attitude improved as well. When I saw her three weeks after her initial visit, she was perkier and had gained a few pounds. She still had some muscle wasting over her spine, but I wasn't concerned about this as she was feeling better. Of course the swelling in her abdomen did not decrease in size, but her abdominal tumor did not seem to be growing. I instructed Linda to continue with the supplements as directed. She stopped the oxazepam as Shasta was eating normally on her own. I asked Linda, who now was thrilled that Shasta was slowly improving, to update me weekly on her progress and to call if there were any concerns.

Linda reported weekly as requested. Shasta continued to feel better, eat well, and in Linda's enthusiastic words, she was "acting like a puppy again!" Linda was thrilled that Shasta was feeling better and had begun to rally. This made me feel good, and reinforced my decision to offer Linda a treatment plan that I had never tried on any other pets. I had no idea whether these therapies would actually work for Shasta, but I was thrilled to hear that she was responding to her treatments.

I often hear from pet owners that their pets regain a lot of their youthful vim and vigor when using natural therapies, even when the pets have a disease that ultimately will be fatal. One of the good side effects from a holistic approach is that even when we don't win the war against the disease, for a time the pet experiences healing. "Feeling good" goes along with healing, and owners are thrilled that pets, formerly lethargic, act like puppies and kittens again.

While I was very happy to hear that my care of Shasta was resulting in improvement, deep down I knew it was a matter of time before her horrible disease would overcome Shasta's healing. I didn't know how much time Shasta had before the cancer would fight back, so I continued to encourage Linda with her care of Shasta.

Shasta continued to do well but, sadly, her recovery was not to last long. Almost three months after starting her integrative treatment, Shasta started feeling ill again. Her appetite declined over the course of two to three days, and she became weak. At that time, Linda and I agreed that Shasta had fought her horrible disease for as long as she could. We humanely decided to intervene with euthanasia so she would not suffer.

We did not reach our goal of keeping Shasta alive until Christmas, but Linda was thankful that we gave Shasta several months of good-quality life. Fortunately, Jason was able to visit with her one weekend while she was feeling well. The time they spent together gave him closure. While I can never know what my animal patients are thinking, I believe that Shasta hung on long enough to say good-bye to Jason, and then, realizing that he was now at peace, stopped her valiant fight and was ready to leave this world quickly and peacefully.

In relating this story of healing to our local cancer specialist, she told me that she was happy we were there to help, as she had never had a patient with this type of cancer live longer than two to three weeks from the initial diagnosis. Shasta's success at battling her liver cancer, while temporary, gave me hope that there really was something to this holistic approach. I, too, had once been skeptical of it, not seeing how herbs and nutritional supplements could have any positive effect on a very sick pet. Having one case such as Shasta improve with these therapies was certainly no guarantee that this holistic approach would work as well or better in future cases. Still, it offered me some hope that I was able to do something for a pet who could not be helped by any conventional therapies, who should've died within a few days following my initial diagnosis of her liver cancer. I was also hopeful that the particular specialist who helped with this case, and who saw the positive influence the holistic approach had on Shasta, would continue to be open to using these modalities in addition to her chemotherapeutic treatments on any future cases I might send to her. I also secretly hoped that the success I had with Shasta might even encourage this specialist and others in our area to refer their patients to me so that I could integrate my holistic therapies with their conventional therapies; we could then offer an even greater chance of successful treatment to many more pets, turning hopeless cases into those in which some hope for improvement, if not an outright cure, would occur.

As you can see, supporting a pet through cancer treatment is not always easy and requires a large commitment of time, energy, and often financial resources. Without pet health insurance to cover the costs, these can easily run into the thousands of dollars for many pet owners. A dedicated owner is needed in order to offer the pet the best possible chance of recovery, cure, or at least an extended, disease-free interval when the cancer is in remission. In veterinary medicine, we usually do not "cure" most cancers (this is also true for most human cancers as well). Our objective is usually to help the pet live as long as possible with the cancer, and enjoy an acceptable quality of pain-free life. As such, we all define success differently. For some, it is only when a disease is cured, but for many others, success means we delay death, and the owner continues to enjoy a quality life with the pet. Linda and I both agreed that even though we did not cure Shasta, we accomplished our goals and were successful. We both felt that we had done everything for her, and felt good that we had tried something when everyone else had given up on her. I was honored that I was given the chance to participate in the care of Shasta, and told Linda that I appreciated her confidence in me, which inspired me to do all that I could for her beloved pet.

At the time of Shasta's diagnosis, I did all I knew to help her fight her cancer. Now it's ten years later, and I've learned a lot more. I have many more therapies to help my cancer patients live comfortably and longer with their malignancies. I've actually written a book teaching pet owners and veterinarians how to combine natural and conventional cancer therapies (*The Natural Vet's Guide to Preventing and Treating Cancer in Dogs*), and our success rate is very impressive in healing most pets with cancers.

Still, we all remember our first cases. I am glad Linda didn't want to give up and was willing to try anything to help Shasta, and I'm certainly glad this first attempt at using integrative medicine to treat a cancer patient was successful. While Shasta, unfortunately, did not live until the Christmas holidays, she lived almost three months, unheard of for pets with terminal liver cancer diagnosed very late in the course of the disease.

Shasta was my second case using integrative medicine. Like my success with Brittany and her allergies, Shasta's response to therapy gave me the impetus to continue learning everything I could and trying as many therapies as possible to help heal my patients.

Juno

More recently, I've had a case of liver cancer in a cat. Compared with dogs, cats rarely get liver cancer, and I hardly ever diagnose this problem in my feline patients. This particular cat's situation was even more dire than the one presented by Shasta. Juno, a fifteen-year-old rex cat, had been healthy his entire life, so imagine what a shock it was for his owner to find out that Juno had suddenly developed a life-threatening problem. Juno was diagnosed with a liver mass by his regular veterinarian, after examining him for the complaint of "not feeling well." The doctor, realizing he couldn't help him, wisely referred Juno to the local cancer specialist for evaluation. A liver mass is rarely a good thing for a pet to have; most are cancerous, and those that aren't still require a lot of treatment. Fortunately, an ultrasound examination, one of the tests performed by the cancer specialist that is commonly done for pets with abdominal cancer, showed the possibility of the tumor being confined to just one part of his liver, which meant surgical removal might be an option and possibly even curative.

Juno's owner, Jane, loved this little cat, and money was no object when it came to his care. Even though Juno was advanced in age, Jane wanted to give him any chance that might help him recover. I appreciated her perseverance. Unfortunately, I see far too many pets whose owners are discouraged from pursuing aggressive therapies by veterinarians who consider these pets too old to treat. While age is certainly one of many factors that must be taken into consideration when deciding upon the appropriate treatment for a pet, no pet is too old for proper care. Most of my practice is composed of geriatric pets, and their owners all want them to live to be a hundred years old! Pet owners know that I will recommend the best therapy regardless of age, as I do not believe any pet should be deprived of the proper therapy simply because someone else feels that it is too old. As a result of her dedication to Juno, Jane decided to try surgery if it offered any hope of curing her special little friend.

The surgeon to whom Jane was referred was able to remove most of the tumor, but unfortunately, a small piece of it was in a location that was inoperable, being tangled up in a large mass of important blood vessels. This meant he had to leave a part of the mass behind in Juno's abdomen. Still, he felt good that he got most of the mass, which should have helped Juno live longer since he had less cancer to fight.

The biopsy of the liver mass that was surgically removed did indicate that it was cancerous as was expected by all of the doctors treating Juno. Unfortunately, Juno experienced a very rare side effect from his cancer surgery. The remaining small amount of cancerous liver tissue that could not be removed grew so rapidly that within one week after his surgery it was almost as large as his original tumor! A follow-up ultrasound showed that Juno only had about 10 percent of normal liver remaining to function, and no patient can live with that.

This is a tragic but, thankfully, almost unheard-of side effect when treating cancer surgically. While removing most of a cancerous mass is usually beneficial to the pet, as it leaves less cancer behind for other therapies to attack, at times something goes terribly wrong. When most of the cancer is removed, some strange signal is given to the few remaining cancer cells to re-produce quickly, literally overnight. This new, rapid growth of cancer is very aggressive, even more so than the original cancer that was removed, and usually no therapy can help kill this uni-formly resistant and aggressive mass of cancer cells. Cancer that grows this quickly and aggressively usually results in a death sentence within a few days.

I explained to Jane that her beloved Juno, weakly lying on his favorite white and blue satin pillow during our visit, barely able to lift his head, was in a very bad way. I reassured her that she and the other doctors had done everything correctly, literally following the textbook in removing most of the cancer and in treating Juno, but that the cancer that had grown within days of his surgery would be difficult if not impossible to kill. Looking at poor Juno, weak from his cancer and recent liver surgery, I would not have blamed Jane if she decided to give up and hu-manely euthanize him. Still, I am the source of last resort for my clients, and Jane wanted to explore all hopeful possibilities before finally deciding no more could be done for him. She felt that Juno had come so far in dealing with this cancer; until he was ready to give up, *she* would not give up and would continue to assist him in his fight with this deadly disease. While it was hard to look at poor Juno, quietly lying on his pillow, I admired Jane's desire to fight for him.

My aggressive protocol for Juno included the following med-ications and supplements.

Prednisone is a steroid commonly used in cancer patients to reduce inflammation that often occurs with tumors. Prednisone can often kill some cancer cells as well. Its well-known side effect of "making the pet feel better" was also a great reason to try it on Juno.

I also dosed him heavily on supplements designed to strengthen his immune system and boost any remaining liver function. These included ONCO Support and Hepato Support from Rx Vitamins *for* Pets, and Detox-Kit from Heel to cleanse his system.

Jane, through her Internet research, also asked about putting Juno on other supplements she had found that might help patients with cancer, including Poly MVA and Transfer Factor. She also inquired about intravenous vitamin C therapy, as she had read that it might help some cancer patients. As I explained to Jane, I was comfortable with any of these additional treatments even if I didn't routinely use them as part of my normal cancer protocols. If Jane wanted to try these additional treatments to help Juno, I was all for it.

There are many wonderful cancer therapies, and no veterinarian can possibly use all of them on every pet. As long as pet owners run things by me, I'm never opposed to their adding other therapies, conventional or alternative, to my prescribed treatment. My main fear is that an owner will stop using a therapy I prescribe, relying instead on some quackish cure-all supplement someone is hawking to make a few bucks. By keeping me abreast of any additional therapies owners wish to try on a dying pet, we can work together to make sure everything we use is safe, nontoxic, and has the best chance of actually doing some good for the pet.

While Jane was very attentive to Juno and obviously wanted to offer him every possible chance for recovery, I couldn't help but notice during our visit that Jane really didn't grasp the severity of Juno's illness. He was dying, and would in all likelihood die within days from his aggressive cancer no matter what I or anyone else tried to do for him. I didn't think it was a stubborn refusal to give up. She just wasn't prepared to process her pet's horrible situation. The treatment that should have bought him more time not only failed to do so but also made him worse, and she wasn't quite ready to face that reality.

While I always want to be realistic with a pet owner whose beloved friend is facing what appears to be imminent death, I've learned that "reality" is often hard to define when it comes to healing. What appears to be the case often turns out better (or sometimes worse) than expected. Still, since no one has final control over how a case will turn out, I think the best approach for me is to offer hope while still making sure the owner knows the worst-case outcome. Anything could happen to Juno, but Jane didn't seem to grasp (or want to grasp) that things really did seem pretty darn hopeless. Jane was still stuck in the denial phase of grieving, and nothing I could say would help her move out of this phase and accept Juno's condition. I did all I could do to be supportive of her and knew that soon she would come to accept the reality of the situation.

The good news is that despite the odds against him, Juno did improve temporarily. I knew that the likelihood of him functioning on 10 percent of his normal liver function was small, and that the aggressive nature of his cancer made it highly unlikely that anything I could do for him would make a difference in the long term. However, thanks to a persistent owner who was willing to do everything we could both come up with to help Juno, he did have a few good months of life in him. Like Shasta, he was never cured of his extremely aggressive cancer. Still, he got to spend an extra four months with Jane, who loved him to the very end.

Chanel

Chanel is one of many pets I've never actually seen in person but have helped through a tough illness. When her owner, Mona, came for her initial consult, she didn't bring Chanel as the dog had recently been diagnosed with liver cancer. Not only was Chanel not feeling well enough to travel for several hours to my office, but also visiting the veterinarian was not one of her favorite activities. Since she had just been through several veterinary visits and quite a bit of poking and prodding, I totally understood and didn't blame Mona for leaving Chanel to enjoy the quiet solitude and comfort of her home.

Chanel was a nine-year-old spayed female, a beautiful white American Eskimo dog who, according to Mona, was "the prettiest Eskimo I've ever seen." Even though Chanel had never experienced any serious health problems for most of her life, she had the misfortune to be diagnosed with liver cancer one month prior to this consult. According to Mona, Chanel was feeling fine and had gone to her doctor for a routine checkup and a dental cleaning to treat Chanel's periodontal disease. During this checkup visit the doctor performed blood testing to make sure that it would be safe to put Chanel, an older pet, under anesthesia for the dental cleaning. I was happy to hear this, as many doctors do not routinely do any sort of screening prior to anesthesia. It's imperative to do a proper preanesthetic evaluation (unless the pet is so uncooperative as to make it impossible to do any type of examination or laboratory testing without sedation) to make sure the pet doesn't have any other problems prior to anesthesia. Sometimes the anesthetic or surgical procedure is postponed due to findings from the examination or laboratory testing; other times the anesthetic regimen needs to be changed to compensate for abnormal findings. In Chanel's case, the presurgical laboratory evaluation caused her dental cleaning to be canceled, as the veterinarian discovered elevated liver enzymes on her blood profile.

After canceling Chanel's dental procedure, her doctor did an ultrasound examination to see if he could find a reason for the elevated liver enzymes. This exam showed that Chanel had a mass in her abdomen in the area of the liver, which likely caused the liver enzymes on her blood profile to elevate. Exploratory surgery was scheduled for the following day to determine the cause of the mass and to see if it could be removed.

Not only did the surgeon find spots presumed to be cancerous on several liver lobes, but Chanel also had a very large spleen that contained a few nodules as well. The spleen was removed due to the high suspicion of it being cancerous, and several biopsies were done on the affected liver lobes. Thankfully, due to a great job by the surgeon, Chanel survived her surgery and recovered quickly.

While the surgery went very well, the results from her biopsies were not as positive. The pathologist reported that although the tumors in the spleen were benign, the liver biopsy showed a type of cancer that commonly affects the liver called adenocarcinoma. Due to the advanced nature of her liver cancer and the general lack of responsiveness to conventional therapies for this type of cancer, none were recommended for Chanel, and a poor prognosis was given. Mona was told to go home, enjoy whatever time Chanel had remaining, and prepare for the worst.

Mona and her husband, Peter, were not prepared for this bad news and were devastated. A few days after they took Chanel home, one of their neighbors, who often babysat Chanel when Mona and Peter went on vacation, happened to see Mona outside playing with Chanel and began talking with her. Mona sadly related to her Chanel's bad diagnosis and hopeless prognosis. At the time her neighbor was an avid fan of my weekly newspaper column. She told Mona about me, explaining my holistic philosophy. While there are never any guarantees, the neighbor thought that I might be able to help Chanel and insisted that Mona make an appointment with me before giving up. Although Mona didn't believe anything would help Chanel based upon the grave prognosis she had been given, her neighbor was so insistent that an integrative approach might offer some hope that Mona called our office and scheduled an appointment.

When I heard Mona explain Chanel's story, I knew that this would be another tough case, like Shasta and Juno. It's extremely unlikely that any pet, no matter how healthy it is otherwise, can live very long with a diagnosis as tragic as Chanel's. I wanted to help, but I also had to be realistic with Mona.

After reviewing the records Mona had brought with her for this visit, I asked her about Chanel's diet. She told me that Chanel was currently eating several natural foods, including

Wysong, Wellness, and Solid Gold. Mona also told me that Chanel had not had any recent vaccinations, which I was happy to hear. So many veterinarians go ahead and give a pet vaccinations even after a diagnosis of cancer. This serves no purpose, and may cause the cancer to grow and spread faster. Thankfully, since Chanel's veterinarian had not vaccinated her, this was one less thing that would require treatment.

Mona also told me that Chanel's veterinarian had prescribed a drug called Metacam, an NSAID, usually prescribed to relieve pain in surgical patients and to relieve pain and inflammation in pets with arthritis. Many doctors are now prescribing NSAIDs for patients with cancer as research suggests that these drugs may slow the growth and spread of cancer. Most oncologists prefer to prescribe the NSAID piroxicam as it was the first NSAID discovered that inhibited the growth and spread of cancer. In fact, a few rare anecdotal reports described cancer totally disappearing in pets taking piroxicam. While I have never seen this happen, I believe that piroxicam has the potential to help pets with cancer and usually prescribe it for these patients. Other than the Metacam, Chanel's doctor had not prescribed anything else to help her fight her cancer.

I knew that my cancer-therapy program would have to be very aggressive if there was to be a chance of offering Mona any hope at all for Chanel. I told Mona that I could not even guess how long Chanel might live with the treatment, but that I was going to do everything possible to help her live as long and comfortably as possible.

Mona was very grateful for my honesty and appreciative of my desire to help her and Chanel. She was willing to try anything to give her special friend hope against what appeared to be totally hopeless odds in fighting off a disease that was usually 100 percent fatal within a few weeks following a diagnosis.

Here's what I prescribed for Chanel. I switched her from Metacam to piroxicam. In addition to this therapy, I prescribed a low dose of doxycycline, an antibiotic usually used to treat various infections in people and pets. Like piroxicam, it also has been shown to slow down the growth and spread of cancer. It appears to do this by inhibiting certain enzymes that cancers need to spread from their point of origin throughout the body.

To help detoxify Chanel's body, I prescribed the homeopathic remedy called Detox-Kit from Heel. I like to use this remedy for all of my cancer and chronically ill patients as I feel that detoxifying and cleansing the body assists in the healing process. The remedy consists of three separate vials of homeopathic medicine, and it is easily administered in the pet's drinking water. To help assist her immune system in fighting off the growth and spread of her cancer, I prescribed three supplements. The first is a favored herbal supplement called ONCO Support by Rx Vitamins *for* Pets. This is a powerful cancer remedy, made up of several potent herbs that strengthen the immune system, support the gastrointestinal tract, and support the liver as it detoxifies waste products from the cancer cells and assists the body in detoxifying from chemotherapy drugs.

I also prescribed a potent antioxidant called Super-Ox from Nutri-West. Antioxidants are useful in preventing further cell damage in pets with cancer.

I also prescribed a Chinese herbal formula from Evergreen Herbs called Immune+. This product was one of the first herbs

I ever used in treating pets with cancer, and it still remains one of my favorite choices to boost the immune system and help the pet feel better.

To help support Chanel's damaged liver I prescribed two herbal supplements, a liquid called Liv-GB from Nutri-West, and an herbal remedy from Rx Vitamins *for* Pets called Hepato Support. These two products, which contain herbs and vitamins to help heal the damaged liver, including milk thistle and B vitamins, are well-known liver supplements.

With this combination of remedies to support Chanel's immune system, fight off the cancer, reduce further cell damage, and support her damaged liver, there was at least a little bit of hope that we would be able to get Chanel and Mona some quality time with each other before she eventually succumbed to her terrible disease.

I truthfully didn't expect to hear a great report when I called Mona several weeks after our initial consultation. Most pets with this type of cancer are lucky to live even a few weeks with an aggressive supplement routine. Shasta was my first case with this type of cancer to defy the odds and to live several months. Even today, with my increased knowledge in treating pets with this type of cancer, and even better supplements that are now available to help these pets, many still do not live as long as I would like due to the advanced nature of their cancer when first diagnosed. Early screening, done by regular examinations and laboratory testing, including blood and urine, is so essential in trying to identify pets with aggressive cancers, as early diagnosis plus aggressive therapy allow the best chance for a long, healthy life.

Consequently, I was surprised when I spoke to Mona and

she said that Chanel was doing great! Chanel was her happy old self and never acted like she was sick at all. In fact, Mona's neighbor, who had originally referred her to me, was shocked when she saw Mona and Chanel on their daily walk just a few days following the start of the therapy I had prescribed. She was simply stunned to see that Chanel was not acting like a dog who was diagnosed with a fatal disease and had been given only days or weeks at the most to live.

The good news is that it's been almost four years since Chanel was first diagnosed with her fatal disease. Mona tells us that she's doing fantastically, still taking her supplements, and still beating her cancer. While it's hard to say exactly why Chanel has done so well, to me it's nothing short of miraculous. Obviously a combination of our integrative therapies, coupled with her strong will to live and her own innate healing ability, has provided a positive outcome. Regardless of the exact reason for her cure, Mona and I were elated at her unexpected recovery.

Even though her healing was totally unexpected, my entire health-care team shares in Mona's joy and delight in the realization that Chanel, given up for dead by everyone, has beaten the odds and has been cured of her incurable cancer.

Buddy

Of course, before a pet owner ever gives up hope for a pet with liver cancer, or any type of cancer, it's imperative that the diagnosis of "cancer" is correct, for it is crucial in order to prevent the hopeless scenario that some pet owners find themselves in.

Buddy was a great looking and extremely outgoing Blenheim-coat color pattern, Cavalier King Charles spaniel. These dogs, often confused with their similar-looking relative, the cocker spaniel, are among the happiest breeds in the canine kingdom, and Buddy was no exception. Long-legged with flowing feathering on his four legs, representative of the breed, Buddy greeted me with a lot of enthusiasm as I entered the room and began my visit with him and Melissa, an attractive young lady I estimated to be in her mid twenties.

It's often said that many pet owners resemble their pets, and this was certainly a good example. Melissa was a tall woman, about five-foot-ten, with hair that freely flowed down to about the middle of her back. Her smile, like Buddy's happy attitude, was contagious. They made the perfect pair.

Unfortunately, their visit was not for a happy reason. As Melissa explained, five-year-old Buddy was her best friend, a gift from her dad shortly before he passed away a few months prior to this visit. Unlike her former boyfriend, who was not supportive during the difficult time she experienced upon her dad's passing, Buddy was always there for her, licking her face and hands and snuggling with her as she struggled to cope with her grief over her father's death. A few weeks before this visit, Buddy had seen his doctor for an annual checkup and vaccines. During the physical examination, the doctor felt a mass in Buddy's abdomen. He told Melissa that he was 99 percent sure that Buddy had cancer, and that nothing could be done. Needless to say, this was devastating news to Melissa, who was not prepared to lose another devoted family member at this time.

Shortly after receiving Buddy's death sentence from his regular doctor, Melissa found herself at her local bookstore, researching cancer in dogs. Fortunately, she found my books *The Natural Health Bible for Dogs & Cats* and *The Natural Vet's Guide to Preventing and Treating Cancer in Dogs*. She quickly purchased both books, reading them within days of her purchase. Upon reading my biography, she realized that my office was just minutes from her house. Excited by the potential hope for Buddy after reading my books, she eagerly scheduled an appointment with me.

As I reviewed the medical records she had brought with her, several things struck me as very odd. First, there were really no medical records to speak of regarding Buddy's diagnosis of liver cancer. While it is certainly likely that a dog with an abdominal mass has cancer of either the spleen or the liver, it's never acceptable to offer such a hopeless diagnosis and prognosis without further testing and proof of one's suspicions. Buddy's original doctor should have used the abnormal finding of an abdominal mass as a starting point for more testing, to include at least blood and urine testing and hopefully an abdominal X-ray and ultrasound, and a biopsy of the mass if possible. Instead, nothing was done except simply to proclaim a diagnosis of cancer with no hope for recovery.

Second, despite the doctor's suspicion of an imminently fatal cancer, he still vaccinated Buddy with his full complement of vaccines! Not only do normal, healthy pets not need vaccines each year, but also *no* pet needs every vaccine in the doctor's refrigerator, and only a few pets need most of them. Additionally, unless legally required to do so, pets with cancer should *never* be vaccinated as this can speed up the cancer, bring the pet out of remission, and ultimately make the cancer grow and kill faster.

And even if Buddy had only weeks to live as pronounced by his original doctor, why would a pet on his deathbed need vaccines?

Third, I noticed from the doctor's barely legible scribbling on the medical records that Buddy did not have any clinical signs of cancer during his visit. While it is certainly possible that the doctor found Buddy's cancer before Buddy showed signs of illness, this was just one more piece of the puzzle that didn't make any sense.

I reviewed all of these oddities with Melissa. The more we talked, the less hopeless Buddy's case seemed. I told her it was certainly possible that Buddy's tumor might actually be benign and not cancerous. This didn't mean he didn't have a serious disease, only that he might have a problem that could be curable! Melissa's eyes lit up as she realized for the first time that her special friend might not be a few weeks away from death, and might actually be around for many more years.

During his physical examination, I noticed that Buddy did in fact have an abdomen that was larger than I would expect for a dog of his breed and size. When I felt it with my hands, a procedure called palpation, I did feel a large mass on the lower part of his abdomen near the edge of his rib cage. This would certainly make sense if he had a liver tumor. Since there's no way to know if an enlarged liver is cancerous without doing some type of testing, I told Melissa that I would need to do radiographs and, schedule an ultrasound of Buddy's abdomen, followed by a biopsy of his liver tumor. She agreed to bring Buddy back the next day. Before she left, I obtained blood and urine specimens from him to check his liver enzymes and to see if any other health problems might be affecting him. I also sent her home with several supplements to strengthen his liver, letting her know I would probably add more to his regimen pending his ultrasound results. The two I prescribed were Cholodin from MVP Laboratories and Hepato Support from Rx Vitamins *for* Pets, both important in helping the liver detoxify and heal.

When Buddy returned the following day, he underwent two procedures; the first test that needed to be done was to take radiographs of his chest and abdomen. The abdominal radiographs would help outline the extent of his tumor. The chest radiographs are necessary for every cancer patient in order to screen for metastatic disease, or the spread of cancer. Since many cancers metastasize (spread) via the blood or lymphatic vessels to the chest, it's vitally important to check for additional tumors in the lungs before starting therapy. While natural supplements can often help even those patients whose disease has progressed so far as to have already spread, once metastatic disease is detected most oncologists will not administer chemotherapy as it is unlikely to be of much value.

Buddy, unlike many patients, was very cooperative during the radiographic procedure and did not require sedation. Although two radiographs of the abdomen were deemed sufficient, it's always important to take three views of the chest (one on each side and one as the pet lies on his back or chest), as lung tumors may fail to appear on two views but show up on the third. Fortunately, Buddy's chest radiographs were free of obvious cancerous lesions, and nothing unexpected showed up on his abdominal films.

Following his radiographs I had our local specialist perform an ultrasound on Buddy's abdomen to further delineate the extent of his disease, as well as to biopsy the tumor to determine if it was benign (as Melissa and I hoped) or malignant. Buddy was gently laid on his side and the specialist applied the ultrasound probe to his abdomen. His internal organs quickly appeared on the screen of the ultrasound machine, and it took only a matter of seconds before the specialist was able to find his liver tumor with the ultrasound probe. It was quite large, but was thankfully only confined to one liver lobe rather than involving his entire liver, as is so typical with liver cancer in dogs and cats. The good news was that no other lesions were seen in his remaining liver lobes or any other abdominal organs. This increased the possibility of the tumor being benign. Following the ultrasound examination I gave Buddy a mild sedative and local anesthetic so that a biopsy needle could be passed, using the ultrasound probe for guidance into the liver tumor, and a tiny amount of tissue was removed and sent to the pathology laboratory for diagnosis. Buddy quickly recovered from his sedative and was no worse for wear.

I told Melissa the good news: that the tumor only involved one lobe of Buddy's liver, and that no other tumors were seen in his abdomen or chest. We were both hopeful that the biopsy would prove benign, but I told Melissa the results would take about two to three days before we knew the answer. I assured her not to panic and think the worst, but I knew she was in for a few tense days, praying for the good news she really wanted. It's never easy for an owner to have to wait for an answer that literally can mean life or death, but I told her that no matter what the results were, we would work together to do our best to keep her special companion alive, healthy, and happy for as long as possible. She knew I had Buddy's best interest at heart, and I knew that no matter what, she would provide Buddy with the best care any pet could desire. I hugged her as we parted and told her I would call her as soon as I knew something.

My receptionist got the biopsy report first, as it came over the fax machine located by the left side of her desk. She knew I wanted to know the results as soon as they came in, so she rushed them back to me as I sat at my desk completing a phone call with another pet owner. The smile on her face gave me a heads up that the news for Buddy was positive. Quickly skimming the fax as I finished my phone call, my eyes darted down to the bottom of the page to the section labeled CLINICAL DIAGNOSIS. It told me that Buddy's tumor was a benign hepatoma, not nearly as common as its more malignant cousin, the adenocarcinoma, but certainly a more welcome diagnosis. This was good news indeed, but it wasn't a clean bill of health, either.

I quickly dialed Melissa's home number, hoping she would be there so she could hear the great news directly from me rather than from a message left on an answering machine. I was glad when she answered the phone after the second ring.

I told her that I had very good news: Buddy's liver tumor was benign and not cancerous. Her response, "Oh, thank God," and a huge burden was lifted from her shoulders. Her lovable companion, given up for dead by her prior doctor who diagnosed cancer without the benefit of any testing, did not face the imminent death Melissa had been led to believe was inevitable. Instead, the diagnosis was a new ray of hope for her and Buddy. I also informed her that except for a moderate elevation of his liver enzymes, which I expected, the rest of his blood and urine testing was normal, giving her yet another piece of good news.

I did tell her that although we still had work to do, I was cautiously optimistic that I, working with the surgical specialist I would refer Buddy to, could in fact offer more than hope for him: we could offer him a totally normal life!

I never like to second-guess or criticize another doctor, but it's obvious that Buddy's original veterinarian did not do a very good job in treating him. Had Melissa followed his advice, Buddy would be dead. I get very upset when I see cases like this. Far too many pets are misdiagnosed or mistreated by far too many doctors. Unless the owner questions the original grim diagnosis and prognosis, the pet's life will be needlessly cut short. It's easy for me to become frustrated, knowing how many pets I and my colleagues who practice integrative medicine can help if the pets are lucky enough to have owners who make their way to our practices. I don't even want to think about just how many animals are caught up in a system that might needlessly condemn them to unnecessary suffering, pain, and ultimately death. There is another way, a much better way that offers hope.

After my call with Melissa, outlining what I had planned to heal Buddy of his benign liver tumor, I called up one of my favorite surgeons in town, Dr. Thomas Fisher. Dr. Fisher D.V.M., A.C.V.S., or Dr. F. as he is called by his adoring clients, is a whiz at surgery. This man can do miracles with a scalpel blade, and has helped many of my patients that even I thought had inoperable conditions. Not only is he a whiz with his knife, but he won't do surgery unless he's absolutely sure it's the best course of action. When he says surgery is needed to help a patient, you can believe him. While not skilled in naturopathic medicine, he is very open to doing whatever it takes to get a patient better. He has even referred a few cases to me to help with postoperative recovery and healing from some pretty devastating conditions, including various cancers.

I began my call with Dr. F. by outlining Buddy's case. I explained the whole story to him, and told him that Melissa really wanted to pursue surgery if he thought he could remove Buddy's tumor and offer him any hope for a cure. Dr. F. told me that he had done surgeries like this before, and that his chance of curing Buddy really depended upon how accessible the tumor was when he got in there to remove it. Based upon the ultrasound results that I had sent him, however, he thought he should be able to remove most, if not all, of the tumor, so he wanted to meet Melissa and Buddy and outline the steps he needed to take to help them.

This was more positive news indeed, and Melissa was happy to hear that Buddy, once given up for dead by his prior doctor, might actually have a chance to be cured! She made the appointment with Dr. F. for evaluation, crossing her fingers that this whole ordeal would soon be over.

After her visit, Dr. F. called to tell me that he and Melissa agreed to do the surgery to remove Buddy's liver tumor. While Melissa knew that the extent of the tumor and Dr. F's ability to remove it could not really be determined until he was actually performing the surgery, all parties felt positive about the possibilities of a cure for Buddy. The surgery was scheduled for the next day, so I would wait another twenty-four hours before knowing the final outcome.

The next afternoon Dr. F. called me around 3:30 P.M. He had excellent news to share with me, and stated that he was able to remove the entire tumorous lobe from Buddy's liver. Dr. F. also told me that he didn't see any other lesions anywhere else in Buddy's abdomen, but to be safe he did remove a small piece of healthy liver and a small piece of healthy spleen for a biopsy. Even though the biopsy we took from Buddy under ultrasound didn't show any signs of cancer, Dr. F. thought it wise to send a big piece of the tumor to be checked for cancer, and I agreed with his assessment.

When I spoke with Melissa that night she told me everything had gone well and was really thrilled that Dr. F. was able to remove Buddy's entire tumor. Buddy was resting comfortably from his liver surgery, and thanks to the analgesic medications Melissa had given him with his dinner, he was not experiencing any pain. She still had a bit of fear while waiting for the biopsy results, but Dr. F. reassurred her that they would probably come back as a benign tumor, based upon its appearance during surgery and the prior biopsy obtained during Buddy's recent ultrasound examination.

Two days later I got another report by fax, this one from Dr. F.'s office, confirming everyone's hopes. No cancer was found on any of the biopsy specimens Dr. F. took during Buddy's tumor surgery, which meant Buddy was now cured of his disease! Dr. F. noted in the fax that he had already shared the good news with Melissa, who was extremely grateful to him for curing Buddy and giving him a second chance at a great life with her.

I spoke with Melissa shortly after receiving the fax, sharing her excitement over the great news about Buddy. Here we had a pet that was doomed for death just a few weeks ago, and now he was cured of the problem that was predicted to be his downfall due to the diligence of a very loving, caring owner.

Although Buddy no longer had a liver tumor, I told Melissa that I still wanted to prescribe several supplements for him. While he didn't have cancer, something in his system allowed his liver to function abnormally and develop a tumor. Conventional medicine doesn't have the tools to address a situation like this, but I knew that the natural approach to health could offer a lot for Buddy.

I proposed that Melissa continue to use the two liver supplements I had previously prescribed. I also added some additional supplements to help detoxify him and strengthen his immune system. I told Melissa that I wanted to prescribe the homeopathic remedy, Detox-Kit, from Heel. This would help cleanse his system and rebalance him toward a normal, homeostatic state. I also prescribed the supplement ONCO Support by Rx Vitamins *for* Pets for his immune system. Even though it's a great supplement for cancer patients, and Buddy did not have cancer, I use it whenever a pet has any type of tumor, benign or malignant, or when I need to strengthen a pet's immune system. Melissa agreed that she wanted to do anything possible to heal his damaged liver and immune system and to try to prevent this tumor from recurring. Finally, I told her that for at least the next year I wanted to schedule a follow-up ultrasound of his liver every six months just to make sure the remaining liver did not develop any other tumors.

As of this writing, Buddy is tumor free and living a wonderful life with a very special companion. Melissa is enjoying his company and has found a new boyfriend who has become Buddy's second-best friend, sharing Melissa's love for this special dog. I know that both she and Buddy will have a wonderful life, and I look forward to continue helping him stay healthy for a very long time.

Occasionally a case such as Chanel's or Buddy's turns out much better than either the owner or I could have ever dreamed, but in most cases pets with cancer will die with their cancers rather than be cured. Still, sometimes the best we can hope for with pets like Shasta and Juno is to offer a few lasting, memorable moments with the family. Keeping the terminally ill pet comfortable, happy, and "healthy" for as long as possible is a very worthwhile goal, even when a true cure and recovery cannot occur.

As things have turned out, I've continued to grow the segment of my practice devoted to the integrated healing of pets with cancers. This is fortunate, as cancer is not only the most feared diagnosis for pet owners but also one of the most common. Unfortunately, both human and veterinary doctors around the world are diagnosing cancer in younger patients. It used to be that cancer was mostly a disease of older patients. I now diagnose cancer in pets under one year of age. While we don't know the exact cause, certainly a combination of genetics (especially from breeding pets who should never be bred), administering too many unnecessary vaccines, feeding pet foods loaded with potentially harmful by-products and chemicals, and exposure to numerous environmental toxins all play a role. Fortunately, the holistic approach to health care is designed to help prevent cancer as well as to heal those patients suffering from it, and I am happy to have chosen this approach to my own health care as well as to that of my patients.

Not a day goes by that I don't have the opportunity to intervene with the healing powers of integrative medicine for a dog or cat with cancer. And I continue to see results that are far superior to similar cases treated only with conventional cancer therapy.

A few years after helping Shasta, I would have the chance to treat a wonderful cat that I still have never actually seen but have helped live years beyond his "terminal" diagnosis.

4

Sometimes Help
Is Just a Phone Call Away

BowTie

The date was August 16, 2004. It's my habit to check my appointment schedule each morning as I prepare to start the day. It's my way to mentally plan for all of the patients I will see, and it helps me and the staff make sure the day flows as smoothly as possible. This particular day was starting off simply enough. I had a recheck scheduled for my first appointment for a dog I had seen the prior month with allergic dermatitis. This was followed by two dental cleanings, ending the morning at 11:00 A.M. with a consultation with an owner whose cat was having litter-box-aversion issues, the most common feline behavior problem small-animal doctors see in private practice.

After lunch, during which I take time to answer e-mails and write articles (and books!), I started my afternoon with a phone consultation with someone living many hours away in another state. Phone consults were always easy appointments, and an especially nice way to kick off a busy afternoon. They were done with pet owners living in another city or state (and sometimes country) who were not able to actually come in for an appointment due to the distance between us. Most often the owners who scheduled phone consults did not have the services of a holistic veterinarian in their area and desperately needed help; unfortunately this situation still exists today as there are few truly holistic doctors available to help pet owners. I was honored to be able to give these owners the same hope I gave each person who was able to visit our office. Many times, these owners were equally if not more desperate for help due to the severe nature of their pets' ailments, the hopeless prognosis given to them by their local veterinarians, and the lack of anyone close by to help them.

These appointments were easier than an in-person visit for many reasons. The owner didn't have to struggle catching the pet at home, putting it in a carrier (which is not always successful), and then driving to the office, hoping the pet won't become too stressed during the car ride. Often cats become so stressed that they vomit, urinate, defecate, or exhibit some combination of these undesirable behaviors during the ride, which makes for a big mess during the visit. Staff members are then needed to help during an office visit, and if the cat is particularly stressed or aggressive, anesthesia is needed to calm the patient and allow a proper and thorough examination. (By the way, giving a few drops of Rescue Remedy, Composure liquid, or a Nutricalm capsule to the cat, or placing a few drops of lavender oil on a cotton ball in the carrier, can help a lot in calming down a cat or any pet who doesn't like going to the doctor!)

A phone consult, on the other hand, was quite simple. Twenty-four hours prior to the actual consult, the pet owner would fax me pertinent medical records, which we would review together during the phone call. At the appointed time, the owner would call and we would discuss the case for up to thirty minutes without interruption. I would make recommendations for more testing or treatment, and if natural therapies were indicated it was a simple matter of mailing the owner whatever supplements I felt would help the pet heal.

While all of us loved phone consults for these reasons, I think the best reason for a phone consult was simply because there were so few holistic veterinarians available to help pets. Phone consults allowed holistic doctors to treat pets that might otherwise have died when conventional medicine could no longer help. (I used to do many phone consults, but sadly, our Texas State Board of Veterinary Medicine recently changed our rules of professional conduct and no longer allows doctors in Texas to help pets without a live, in-person office visit. While I understand their thinking that nothing can substitute for actually examining the pet, my staff has had to tell many owners living in other states who had no other access to a holistic doctor that I would not be able to help them, either. It saddens me to think of all the wonderful pets who may have died prematurely simply because I was not allowed to spend thirty minutes on the phone with these owners, thirty minutes that could literally mean the difference between life and death for many of these special creatures.)

As so it was that day in August that I was excited to help Cheryl by phone with her concerns about her cat, BowTie, a fifteen-year-old male Maine Coon cat that was in very bad shape. According to Cheryl, BowTie was not eating well, had lost weight (which was quite obvious to Cheryl since Maine Coons are by nature normally very large, big-boned felines), and was lethargic. His most striking clinical sign was an abdomen that was enlarged because of fluid accumulation (a condition doctors term ascites or peritoneal effusion).

No doctor had been able to reach a definitive diagnosis, but all of the generalists and specialists who had evaluated BowTie came to the conclusion that the most likely diagnosis was a very malignant type of cancer called carcinomatosis, the term given to any highly malignant cancer that has spread throughout the abdominal cavity, affecting various organs and the lining of the abdominal cavity and its organs (peritoneum).

After reviewing the records Cheryl had sent me, I also was confident that this was in fact the most likely diagnosis. There are very few diseases that produce abdominal fluid accumulation in cats and dogs, and none of these diseases are good. All of the testing done by the previous doctors had ruled out the other diseases that cause fluid to accumulate in the abdomen such as heart failure, heartworms, and Feline Infectious Peritonitis (FIP) and the pathology report on the fluid removed from BowTie showed cells that were compatible with cancer. Based upon this, all of the doctors who were caring for BowTie determined that the case was hopeless, and no therapy was available that would in any way change the bleak outlook for this wonderful cat.

Based upon the clinical picture that Cheryl and the medical records she provided were painting, I knew this would be a very tough case. I honestly told her that while I could try to help BowTie, if in fact his condition was as bad as she and the doctors described, then I feared that nothing I could do would make a difference.

Looking over the medical records, I saw that Cheryl's doctors had done everything right in their conventional treatment of BowTie. They had used the typical array of medications, including steroids and antibiotics, and fluids were administered to BowTie subcutaneously (under the skin) to keep him well hydrated and to flush out any toxins in his system. Cheryl was even force-feeding him at home to help him maintain his strength and prevent further muscle wasting and weight loss, but nothing really seemed to help him as he continued to deteriorate before Cheryl's eyes.

I'm always discouraged when doctors treat a pet with what appears to be the correct therapies and yet these therapies don't offer even a slight amount of improvement in a patient. Regardless of the disease, most pets will show some improvement with the symptomatic treatment given to BowTie by his conventional doctors. The lack of response to his aggressive supportive care further frustrated Cheryl, adding to the hopeless situation of the case. As we talked, I could hear the desperation in her voice. She loved BowTie and was not ready for him to die.

I knew BowTie would be an especially difficult case to heal, and I didn't have high hopes for him at all. Still, Cheryl told me that she wanted to try anything to save the life of her special companion, and I was willing to throw everything I had at him in a last-ditch attempt to save his life. Either we were going to summon every ounce of healing power he had left within him or his disease would ultimately and quickly win this war.

This is the treatment regimen I prescribed for BowTie: I knew that his underlying problem was a weakened immune system, allowing this rare form of cancer to develop; therefore, I concentrated my efforts on helping his immune system heal and function at its maximum capacity. I also knew that unlike my canine patients, it's often difficult to medicate cats, regardless of whether the treatment is a conventional or an alternative therapy. This complicates treating cats, and with some I must rely on more easily administered conventional medications and I only use a few supplements for cats that are especially challenging to treat. Fortunately for all of us involved in this case, BowTie was not one of these difficult cats to treat, which made my decision easier regarding which therapies might offer the most help.

I selected Engystol and Echinacea compositums made by Heel. Both are homeopathic remedies that stimulate the pet's immune system, activating the body's defenses to fight off infection, parasites, and cancers. Immuno Support by Rx Vitamins *for* Pets is a wonderful herbal prescription remedy that also helps the pet maintain a strong immune system in its fight against disease-causing pathogens and cancers. I like to combine both herbs and homeopathics in many cases, especially those like BowTie, in which I need to do everything possible to help the pet fight off its disease. Herbs work similarly to drugs and are very potent in their actions, whereas homeopathics are a milder form of natural medicine, relying on the body's energetics that heal from within. The products from Heel, while still milder in action than many herbs, are potent stimulators of healing, even at the cellular level, detoxifying the patient and removing disease as the patient heals.

Omega-3 fatty acids (fish oil) are indicated in just about any health disorder. Their active constituents, EPA and DHA, do many wonderful things for the pet. In cases of cancer, they slow down the growth and spread of the cancer. High doses of EPA and DHA are needed. Cheryl, who was an avid reader of the books I had written on natural pet care, had already begun supplementing BowTie with her own fish oil supplement based upon my suggestions in my award-winning book, *The Natural Health Bible for Dogs & Cats*. BowTie liked the flavor of the product Cheryl was using, which was important, as many dogs and cats have a taste aversion to some of the human supplements that owners often give them, which is one reason I tend to prefer pet supplements for pets and people supplements for people. Cheryl was doing a great job so far, and I liked the particular brand of supplement she was giving BowTie. I instructed her to increase the dosage so it would be more potent and do a better job of controlling BowTie's aggressive cancer.

Finally, antioxidants are very important in treating any disease, especially cancer. They reduce inflammation and cellular oxidation (damage), both of which we suspect probably are the inciting causes of most if not all chronic diseases like cancer. The particular product I prescribed was Proanthozone by Animal Health Options.

I once again reviewed the difficult nature of the case with Cheryl. First, BowTie was an older cat. Older pets have more chronic diseases, as their immune systems usually do not function as well as they do in younger pets. Second, even if we could help him, as an older pet he was nearing the end of his life expectancy. Most doctors suggest that cats live twelve to fifteen years, and BowTie was fifteen. In our practice, when owners use integrative medicine to prevent and treat disease, most cats will live fifteen to twenty years. I reminded Cheryl that BowTie was like an eighty-year-old person. Some people live to eighty-one, and a few make it to a hundred. Therefore, BowTie could die during treatment simply due to old age even though his disease was in remission.

I didn't share this with Cheryl to discourage her from treating BowTie, as I believe too many veterinarians (and medical doctors) aren't aggressive with their recommendations for geriatric patients. This is unfortunate, since older patients have more of these devastating disorders than do younger pets and require similar therapies. I'm a big believer in treating these older pets regardless of their problems, and I enjoy treating our geriatric patients, for they are my greatest success in restoring them to the health they experienced when they were younger. Because so many doctors seem to give up on them due to their advanced age or the cost of treatment, their owners are especially grateful at my enthusiasm in helping their pets regain youthful vim and vigor and in extending their lives. Cheryl, like many of my clients, told me that she wanted BowTie to live "to be a hundred!" I knew she was not discouraged by our conversation but rather encouraged that someone would take her concerns seriously, honestly evaluate BowTie's disease, and still offer to try something to save her special friend despite the overwhelming odds against success.

Finally, Cheryl and I were both aware of the very serious nature of BowTie's illness. Based upon all of the testing that had been done, we knew we were treating what should be an imminently fatal disease. Due to the grave prognosis given by his other doctors, none of them held out any hope or even offered end-of-life hospice care to keep him comfortable until his passing. Cheryl was a committed, extremely loving, and devoted owner who on her own began force-feeding BowTie and keeping him well hydrated by giving him fluid therapy at home. None of this is easy on an owner, but Cheryl truly loved BowTie and never complained. While I knew I was faced with a huge challenge not only in trying to keep BowTie alive as long as possible but also in trying to restore him to normal health, I knew that both Cheryl and BowTie had the harder jobs of going through everything that would be needed to give this grand cat a fighting chance at life.

Fortunately, due to Cheryl's diligence and patience, and BowTie's ability to summon up all of his nine lives, he responded amazingly and very rapidly to the natural therapies I originally prescribed for him. Within one week of our phone consult, Cheryl reported that he was feeling better, eating on his own, and had gone from the brink of death to acting almost totally normal again!

I first began helping BowTie heal from his horrible affliction almost three years ago. A recent phone call from Cheryl to refill the supplements that have helped keep BowTie alive and well confirmed that he is living a healthy, happy life. Asked what she thought of BowTie's success, she responded in her own enthusiastic words, "I just want to shout: It's a *miracle!* I can't thank you enough, Dr. Shawn." Her friends and family members continue to marvel at BowTie's recovery. Even her conventional doctors, while not directly acknowledging that our natural therapies really did any good, are still excited that somehow BowTie is still alive.

· It's hard for me to imagine that this cat, an animal whose prognosis was grim, is still alive and kickin'! Cases like this, which have become quite common in my integrative practice, have convinced me of several facts.

First, it's always important for me to be open and honest with pet owners. I don't ever want to be accused of offering a treatment just to make a few bucks selling some worthless snake oil (as some closed-minded individuals have called natural therapies). I was brutally honest and frank with Cheryl when I evaluated the history she provided and the medical assessments given by BowTie's other doctors. I don't want to be yet another voice proclaiming hopelessness, but I do want to paint an accurate picture of how the average case of a pet with a particular disease is likely to progress. Doing so allows the owner to work with me to make the best determination on how to proceed and how to spend health care funds wisely.

Second, and most important, cases like this continue to impress upon me the magnificent healing power we all possess. I am happy to be wrong in my initial assessment and prognosis when the case turns out in an unexpected but very positive way. Even when my initial hunch might be, "This case really does seem hopeless," I am encouraged by cases like BowTie's to persevere in my efforts, offer anything that might help the pet, and step back and see what happens. No case is too tough to treat, and healing can occur even when the best minds think that "hopeless" is the kindest description of the pet's medical problem. This spirit that moves all of us, both people and animals, is truly amazing in its healing ability. The will to live plus the innate healing ability that resides in every person and pet is indeed very strong and often overcomes even the toughest obstacles. None of us really knows the limits of what our bodies or our pets' bodies can do when it comes to healing, and this is just one of the reasons why I offer healing for all of my patients.

5

Miracles Really Do Happen

Miracles are a funny thing. Everyone seems to have a unique perspective on the subject.

As a Catholic, I do believe that God can choose to intervene in mankind in miraculous, unexplainable ways whenever He chooses to do so. As a doctor/scientist, I am trained to be skeptical of miraculous cures. This healthy skepticism prevents many doctors from supporting every quackish product or healing modality that someone is selling just to make a quick buck. I must always be on guard to protect my patients from faddish therapies that may offer no help and which may in fact be harmful or even deadly.

However, as a holistic doctor I am also open to anything that may offer my patients some benefit, no matter how different or bizarre it seems. I don't always have to know how something works, or why it works, only that it *might* work. While skeptical conventional doctors often wait for proof that a certain therapy works, my patients don't have that luxury. Many are critically ill or injured and need help *now*, not twenty years later when we have proof that a recommended therapy that has already shown effectiveness in clinical practice does in fact work.

Since there are not many resources in the veterinary literature for veterinarians to learn about holistic healing, I subscribe to various holistic medical journals and read textbooks designed to help in the healing of the human species. A number of studies and case reports show the healing, miraculous power of prayer, for example. Many people with advanced, incurable diseases have in fact been cured as the result of intercessory prayer by loving friends and family members. When modern medicine can't explain how a patient heals and an incurable disease disappears, the cure is called "miraculous."

I often tell many of my clients whose pets have serious medical problems that I may not be able to cure their pets, but rather help their pets live as long as possible and enjoy a comfortable, pain-free, happy life with the nonconventional therapies I will use as part of the healing process. I like to tell these pet owners that in order for their pets to actually be cured from their serious afflictions, "I would need a miracle, and I don't get many miracles."

In reality, that's not totally true. I see many miracles every day: Babies are born, our bodies work in complicated and mysterious ways, people learn to forgive themselves and others and to replace hatred with love. The very fact that we can see with our eyes transmitting signals to be interpreted by the visual cortex of our brains is a miracle when you think about how our bodies are put together so wonderfully!

It's just that I don't always see many "miraculous" cures for chronic, often incurable, and sometimes fatal conditions. However, every holistic doctor has favorite cases that defied logic and seemed to exhibit what can only be called miraculous healing. Whether a true miracle occurred from intercessory prayer on the part of the owner who wants a pet to heal, or simply a random act of God, or just the miraculous ability of each patient's body to heal when treated with the right therapies, there are those memorable cases where recovery is even better than expected. This story is an example of such a case.

Jessie

Peter and Angie were a special couple with a special story. My practice is in Texas, but they lived several hundred miles away in a small country town in Louisiana. Having been born and raised in that state myself, albeit in the big city of New Orleans, I always feel a certain kinship to my brethren across the Sabine River. It's important to establish a rapport with my clients at the very start of our relationship; doing so forms a bond of trust and friendship that is an important part of the healing relationship needed to give the pet the best chances for healing. The owners must trust me right from the start, having confidence that I will prescribe the best therapies for their pets. I, too, must have confidence in the owners that their love and concern for their special family member will translate into putting my therapies into action.

I began my visit with Peter and Angie discussing our backgrounds and sharing stories about living in the South, including all of the wonderful native Louisiana foods, like boudin and crawfish, that we enjoyed. I also asked them how they happened to make the trip from a tiny country town in Louisiana to Plano, Texas.

They shared with me that they had read several of my articles on natural pet care and wanted to see if this style of care would be of any help for their pet Jessie. Peter and Angie also told me that one of their friends was a private pilot who had loaned them his services and actually flew them to Texas in his own plane for their visit that day. They were not the first folks who traveled a great distance to see me; many clients make the visit to Texas as there aren't any holistic veterinarians close to them who can offer this form of healing. Some travel hundreds if not thousands of miles across several state lines in an attempt to find a cure for their pet's condition. I am always honored when someone thinks enough of me and my form of medical practice that they will inconvenience themselves by spending several hours on the road (or in the case of Peter and Angie, in the air) to seek my help. This situation always places an extra bit of pressure on me, as I really hope I can help the folks who demonstrate this level of love and commitment to a pet. I don't want their visit to be a waste of time and in vain.

As it turns out, not only were Peter and Angie really nice, down-home Southern folks as I expected, but also their special companion shared this trait. Jessie was a really sweet little red, short-haired three-year-old dachshund that readily approached me when I entered the room and stepped up to the examination table to greet the family. I always take a wait-and-see approach when I enter a room to meet with a pet that I have not previously encountered. Dogs and cats tend to be nervous in a doctor's office, never really knowing what to expect from the visit, but usually sensing that something may not be right. And when you consider that most pets only visit the doctor when they're sick or getting poked, prodded, or stuck with something sharp and painful, it's no surprise that they are not too happy during the visit. Sometimes their trepidation is a reaction to what is also being felt by their owners during the visit. All said, when you consider that most pets don't go to the veterinarian's office just for a fun visit to say hi, I'm not surprised that many pets don't like their visits.

Thankfully, at our practice the opposite is true, as most pets enjoy or at least tolerate their visits without fear. I tend to ignore the patient when I first enter the room, waiting instead for the pet to become comfortable with me before I start petting it. I don't wear a white lab coat, which is intimidating to pets and people alike. Our office doesn't stink with objectionable animal odors like so many other hospitals, as we rely on scented candles and oils, using calming and soothing aromas like vanilla and lavender to create a relaxing, peaceful environment. Also, whenever the owner's schedule allows, we encourage her to stop by at her convenience, simply to say hi, weigh the pet, and give it a treat. These relaxing, quick visits let the pets know that they can come to our office and not always get poked or stuck with something.

It didn't take much time at all for Jessie and me to warm up to each other. While she exhibited all the signs of comfort and happiness in the front end of her body by shaking her head, licking my hands, and exhibiting signs of affection, the rear half of her body did not respond accordingly. Missing were the wiggling trunk and wagging tail we all expect from a happy, friendly pet. Unfortunately, that was the reason Peter and Angie had flown several hours to see me: Jessie was paralyzed from the waist down.

Several months prior to this visit, Jessie had been playing around the house and suddenly let out a loud yelp. When Peter and Angie searched for her to find out what was wrong, they discovered she was dragging her rear legs, unable to stand up and walk on them. They quickly took her to their local small-town veterinarian, who they simply referred to as "Doc." Upon examining Jessie, Doc correctly diagnosed disk disease, more correctly referred to by doctors as intervertebral disk disease (IVDD), a common neurological problem in small animals. The intervertebral disk is composed of a gelatinous core with a tougher outer layer. Certain breeds, such as dachshunds, shih tzus, beagles, and other small breeds, are especially predisposed to having problems with their disks.

If you're going to have one of these breeds, you must be prepared for the likely possibility of back problems—and treating IVDD is not inexpensive: the cost for emergency stabilization and surgery can easily run three thousand to five thousand dollars, which is just one of many reasons I'm a huge fan of pet health insurance for most owners! These breeds are basically born with weakened disks. The weak top part of the disc allows the gelatinous core to bulge (prolapse) into the spinal canal.

This bulging disk puts pressure on the cord and spinal nerves, and this can cause pain, weakness in the limbs, or even sudden total paralysis.

In Jessie's case, her genetically weakened disk quickly broke through its tough outer rim, putting a large amount of pressure on her cord, which caused her to become paralyzed. In many pets, IVDD simply causes some temporary pain that is easily treated with a combination of conventional medications, supplements, and acupuncture. While serious disk problems are rare in most dogs, disk prolapses as severe as Jessie's are true emergencies. The sooner the correct care is given, the greater likelihood of a complete recovery and return to normal walking ability.

Their local veterinarian in Louisiana correctly treated Jessie with steroids, which often work wonders to reduce the swelling seen with this common condition of the nervous system. If all works as expected, the steroids relieve the pressure the extruded gelatinous disk material has placed on the spinal cord and spinal nerves. The affected pet feels better, the pain goes away, and the ability to walk returns shortly, even though the weakened disk remains and could cause problems again in the future. In Jessie's case, however, she was one of the exceptions that did not recover. She no longer experienced pain, but her paralysis continued. At this point, several days after her injury, their regular veterinarian told them he didn't have anything else to offer, so they lived with her paralysis for several months until they read my articles that lead them to our visit.

I asked Peter and Angie why they had not taken Jessie to a surgeon, as I felt that immediate surgery to remove the extruded disk material from Jessie's spinal canal probably would have cured her problem. They stated that their doctor didn't think it would do any good after she failed to respond to the steroids, and that there were no local board-certified surgeons who could do back surgery in their small town.

I was more than a bit frustrated at hearing this. Jessie was a perfect candidate for immediate emergency back surgery at the time of her injury. She was only three years old, in otherwise good health, and was seen by the primary doctor shortly after her injury. Even in a town where there are no board-certified surgeons, Peter and Angie were not that far from their local veterinary school in Baton Rouge where many specialists practice. It's unfortunate that their regular veterinarian wasn't more aggressive in pursuing a referral that could have cured little Jessie.

During my examination, I noted that other than her rear limb paralysis, she was in good health. At this time there was no longer any pain associated with her disk disease, but she did have residual paralysis—what I feared was very likely permanent damage to the nerves that controlled her rear legs, tail, and bladder and bowels. While Jessie could live comfortably the rest of her life in this condition, many owners choose euthanasia rather than deal with the problems that occur in pets with permanent paralysis: a less mobile, less active pet who leaks urine and drops feces throughout the house. Both Peter and Angie assured me they loved their little girl and would not choose euthanasia. They felt they could continue to handle any problems she might exhibit. Still, I really wanted to give them back the pet they once enjoyed, and I knew they really wanted this, too.

I tend not to consider nerve injuries hopeless, permanent, or irreversible until at least one year has passed since the primary injury with no signs of improvement, but I know from experience that the longer the pet has sustained an injury to the nervous system, the greater the likelihood it will not recover any function to that damaged area. Few if any pets recover significant function after four months of complete paralysis if they haven't already shown some healing of the damaged area, especially after failing to respond to their initial treatment.

As a result, I once again found myself having to tell owners who turned to me as their last source of hope that while I was willing to do everything possible to help their pet, the chances of success were greatly diminished because it had been so long since the initial injury, without even a glimmer of improvement in the meantime. While I don't ever consider any case as truly hopeless unless I've tried something to heal the pet, patients like Jessie present an almost insurmountable challenge simply due to the nature of the body's ability to heal. If healing were likely, certainly she would have shown even a little bit of improvement by then, but she had not shown any positive improvement that might give me the idea that her nerves were trying to heal. The good news was that at least her condition had not worsened since her initial back injury and she was pain free, otherwise enjoying her life in Louisiana with Peter and Angie.

Her owners obviously cared for little Jessie, and inconveniencing themselves to make the trip from Louisiana to Texas to help was an awesome expression of their love and concern. They wanted to try anything that might help their sweet friend, and I wanted to give them some glimmer of hope, no matter how desperate things seemed at this initial visit. I literally threw every type of treatment I could think of at Jessie, hoping almost against hope (or at least against logic, knowing the odds were astronomical that this dog would ever regain any significant motor functioning in her rear legs) that something would work and restore Jessie to the very active little dog she had been prior to her injury.

First, I did an electroacupuncture treatment at various points over Jessie's spine. While it would be "textbook correct" to have Jessie return several times each week for continued therapy, I knew that would not be possible. So, after doing the acupuncture treatment, I then demonstrated to Angie and Peter how to do acupressure at home. It's very easy, and basically involves stimulating the same acupuncture points I had chosen with a well-placed finger. I asked them to do the acupressure treatments for thirty to sixty seconds at least twice daily, assuring them it would not hurt Jessie and would be very helpful as part of her therapy. They both told me that this would not be a problem for them, and they were eager to participate in Jessie's care.

I also used several supplements designed to heal the damaged nerves and to support the connective tissues of the spinal column. No conventional medications were needed at that time, as they had already been tried and failed to help Jessie. Instead, I chose natural medicines to help heal her nerves, disks, and supporting connective spinal tissues. Traumeel, a homeopathic by Heel, is useful for any sort of traumatic injury. I combined this natural medicine with another Heel product called Discus compositum, a remedy I've had a lot of success using in disk disease. Traumanex by Evergreen Herbs is an herbal formula also good for any type of traumatic lesions, especially those suffered by pets with disk disease. MegaFlex by Rx Vitamins *for* Pets was also prescribed. I like using joint remedies that contain nutritional factors such as glucosamine and chondroitin, to help heal the connective tissues of the disks and spinal column. While these joint supplements don't heal the nerves per se, they are often an effective adjunctive therapy and help support the surrounding connective tissues. Finally, I prescribed a basic homeopathic remedy called Hypericum, well known for its healing ability in numerous nervous tissue disorders, which I've used with great success in pets with a variety of nervous system disorders.

Trying to be realistic, I also told Peter and Angie about inquiring into getting a dog cart (doggie wheelchair) for Jessie. Several companies make these carts, including K-9 Cart Company, Eddie's Wheels, and Doggon' Wheels. These carts are custom-made for paralyzed dogs and can be lifesaving as they give the dogs the mobility to walk and run that they once had before their paralysis. I was hoping my therapies would work, but I also wanted Peter and Angie to be realistic, knowing that even if Jessie never walked on her own again, the cart would restore her mobility, and they could all enjoy walking and playing with her as they had before her accident.

I also mentioned two other products that might help Jessie. The first was a special bed made by Orange County K9, a company that makes some of the best pet beds I've seen. These beds are made from premium-quality orthopedic memory foam, very soft and comfortable and enjoyed by most pets (my own dog Rita loves hers). They are specially useful to help prevent pressure sores that are often seen in dogs with arthritis or paralysis. I also suggested that Peter and Angie might want to look into static magnets for Jessie. Magnet therapy is often helpful for pets with orthopedic or neuromuscular disease. While there are many companies that make these products, I am most familiar with those made by Nikken.

As the visit ended, I shook Peter's hand, gave Angie a quick hug, and pet little Jessie on her head. I wished them all well, told them to have a safe flight back to Louisiana, and let them know that I would check in with them soon to see how Jessie was doing. I reminded them again to look into ordering a cart for Jessie just in case healing did not occur.

As I do with all of my serious cases, I made a follow-up call to Jessie's owners one month after her initial visit. Sometimes I make calls sooner than that, depending upon the case. Since Jessie was basically a very healthy yet obviously paralyzed dog, there was no reason for an earlier call as I needed to give her nervous system time to try and heal as a result of her prescribed therapies.

I first began the conversation asking Angie if she had yet been able to purchase the specialized cart I had suggested to help give Jessie mobility. I was astounded when she told me that while they had ordered and subsequently received the cart, they did not have a chance to use it as Jessie began walking before her cart arrived!

To say I was astonished is an understatement. Here was a patient, clearly paralyzed for four months after a devastating disk prolapse that damaged her spinal column, who despite the correct use of conventional medications shortly after her dramatic injury, had not even shown the slightest amount of healing during those four months. In such a case, there is little if any hope that the pet will ever regain even partial function of its legs, much less totally return to normal mobility. Yet, somehow, the administration of a few carefully chosen nutritional supplements, coupled with the acupressure treatments her owners administered to her at home, allowed Jessie's nerves to summon up whatever healing power remained in them. It was almost as if she had grown a new spinal cord that functioned without any problems.

This success was more than a simple coincidence. What was once a paralyzed dog was now a totally normal, good-as-new canine that improved so quickly she started walking even before her specially made wheelchair had arrived. All of us, my staff and I, and certainly Peter and Angie, were shocked and thrilled beyond all expectations. Obviously, Peter and Angie's trip to our office was well worth the time and inconvenience. To this day Jessie continues to thrive in the woods of Louisiana, running happily and chasing squirrels as she should, and bringing lots of joy to her loving owners, who continue to follow a holistic approach to keep her healthy.

Jessie is certainly not my first "hopeless" disk injury to experience what I considered a rapid, almost miraculous recovery. My first case occurred several years prior to that meeting and involved a much larger version of Jessie.

Princess

Princess was an eighty-pound, overly enthusiastic bundle of happiness, proudly representing the bassett hound breed. She came tearing into my office for her first visit with us. Despite having a similar condition to Jessie's, Princess's rear-end paralysis certainly didn't slow her down or detract from her "everything's great with the world" attitude toward life.

Her owner, Anita, also sought out my help in dealing with her dog's lack of response to therapy for disk disease. The prior veterinarians who had treated Princess did everything right. Her general practitioner administered steroids immediately following a back injury that caused her to instantly lose motor function of both of her rear legs. He then did the right thing and referred her to our local surgical specialty center. The surgeon, a doctor I've known and respected for many years, did a textbook-perfect dorsal laminectomy spinal surgery to remove her three damaged disks in the middle of her back that were putting pressure on her spinal cord, causing the immediate paralysis seen in Princess following her injury. Her postoperative recovery went well, and she healed quickly from her surgery. Unfortunately, she was one of the very few percentage of dogs that do not regain immediate use of their legs following this commonly performed procedure. Despite the correct diagnosis and treatments, including several grueling weeks of physical therapy after the surgery to help her regain motor function of her legs, Princess just wasn't able to walk, and her back legs remained mostly nonfunctional.

It's not unusual for larger dogs to take longer to recover from back surgery, but by four months of healing time and therapy, Princess should have shown some signs of improvement. As she was failing to improve with conventional therapies, Anita asked the surgeon if he knew of anyone in town that might be able to try something like acupuncture to help her happy-but-still-paralyzed companion. That's when he referred Anita and Princess to our office.

I reviewed with Anita everything that had been done to date with Princess. She understood that Princess already should have shown some improvement, as the surgery was successful and without complications. Anita fully understood that while I would do all I could to help Princess regain at least some function in her rear legs, the case was going to be tough since she had not shown any improvement despite having received outstanding care up to this point. Based upon the history, examination, and consultation with Anita, I decided to treat Princess with a combination of acupuncture, herbs, and homeopathics. I stimulated acupuncture points that were most likely to help the nerves supply motor function to her lower legs. I chose the same natural medicines I used on Jessie to help Princess heal her nerves, disks, and supporting connective spinal tissues. I also instructed Anita how often to administer the remedies, and had her bring Princess back twice weekly over the course of one month to continue her acupuncture therapies.

Within two weeks of starting therapy Princess was already showing signs of improvement. Although she was still dragging her rear legs when she came in for her visit, she was starting to bear weight on them and exhibit voluntary movements. By four weeks, she was almost 100 percent improved! When she came in for her final acupuncture treatment, she was walking on her own, only slipping on her rear legs when she became too excited and raced for the treatment room door to greet me.

After finishing her final treatment, I had Anita continue Princess's oral supplements for another month, and told her to continue to give Princess a supplement called MegaFlex from Rx Vitamins *for* Pets for the rest of her life to provide ongoing joint and connective tissue support. Princess's healing went so well that I've only seen her twice since this visit for a booster treatment with acupuncture when she began to show slight weakness in her rear legs.

I continue to be amazed at how well our pets will heal when the doctor, the pet owner, and the patient work together, don't give up, and let the body do what it can to return to normal function. While there is no guarantee that this level of healing will occur in every case, there is also no guarantee that it *won't* occur. Every pet should be given this opportunity to heal when simply given, and I hope someday all pets will be treated this way, using an integrative approach to remove anything that stands in the way of healing; to administer any other therapies that encourage the body to rid itself of inflammation and remaining tissue damage; and to promote healing of damaged parts that can once again regain the ability to function properly.

As these two cases demonstrated to me, miracles really do happen, and my goal is to give every pet and owner a chance for their own miracles, even when all seems hopeless.

6

Miracles Continue to Happen

I didn't start my journey into holistic care with the goal of saving pets with incurable, fatal diseases. I started using alternative therapies to help all of my pets with allergies that were simply not responding to conventional medications. As I saw the positive responses in these pets, the word began spreading that "Dr. Shawn" was doing something different at his hospital, something that helped pets get better when no one else could help them.

As word spread, more and more people were bringing their pets to me for help. Many of these patients had conditions far worse than allergies, and a lot of them had progressive, fatal, incurable conditions. While I had never planned to treat these conditions, I knew I couldn't turn them away. These pets needed my help, as no one else could offer them anything positive. I was surprised to find how many pets existed with horrible conditions that no one could help. I had seen a number of similar conditions when I was practicing only conventional medicine, but I never really paid attention to how many pets I couldn't help. As I began helping pets with these more serious problems once I began practicing integrative medicine, I sadly began to realize just how many pets had died under my care when I was a conventional doctor because I couldn't offer them any other therapies. Their conditions seemed hopeless. Now I know that those pets did not need to die if only I had discovered holistic medicine earlier. In fact, one of the driving forces that inspires me to teach as many veterinarians and pet owners as I can about holistic medicine is the knowledge that many pets needlessly pass away because no one is able to help them. This is a tragedy that must not continue. Thankfully, more pet owners and veterinarians are opening their minds to using natural care as a way to prevent and treat these horrible, life-threatening conditions.

As my practice has grown, many people have sought my help because they refuse to take no for an answer. These owners do not want to accept that nothing can be done for their pets. In their minds, they wisely want to explore every possible opportunity for healing before they accept a poor or a hopeless prognosis.

Roland

Lloyd and Tina were two such memorable clients. I saw them for the first time several years ago. The reason for their visit that day was their beloved pet Roland, a three-year-old male Bernese mountain dog. For those who haven't seen this wonderful breed, imagine a slightly scaled-down version of a Saint Bernard, without the droopy lips and with much more vivid and striking black, white, and gold colors marking their magnificent bodies. The breed is one of four varieties of Swiss mountain dogs, known in its native land as the Berner Sennenhund, originally developed to work as a draft dog and a watchdog. The Bernese mountain dog is an extremely hardy breed that, like the Saint Bernard, thrives in cold weather. Roland, like many others of his breed, was very friendly. According to Lloyd and Tina, he loved people and was a quick learner.

Roland had been seen by his veterinarian for fairly vague signs, common to a number of diseases but not specific for any one condition in particular. According to the medical records provided by Lloyd and Tina, Roland's original symptoms included lethargy, weakness, drinking excessive amounts of water, urinating excessively, and acting pained when handled in his back and/or abdominal area. He also had multiple firm, cordlike nodules under his skin that were located all over his body. Since his original doctor was perplexed by these unusual symptoms and unable to arrive at a firm diagnosis, he referred Roland to one of our local internal medicine specialists.

Medical records sent to me by that specialist confirmed the findings of the original veterinarian. In addition to the clinical signs noticed by the referring veterinarian, Roland also had a mild fever and continued to exhibit pain when the internal medicine specialist examined his upper and lower abdomen. Since a diagnosis was not apparent from the clinical presentation and history Lloyd and Tina provided the internist, the specialist performed several laboratory tests in an attempt to arrive at a diagnosis.

Radiographs of Roland's abdomen revealed a large mass under his skin on the left side of his abdomen. Aspirates of several nodules on Roland's body were sent to a pathologist for evaluation. It took a few days for the report to come back, but when the pathologist reviewed the aspirates microscopically, he arrived at a diagnosis: malignant fibrous histiocytosis. This disease, commonly seen in the Bernese mountain dog breed, is a very malignant form of cancer. There is no cure for it, and even with aggressive chemotherapy most pets will only live four to six months. Treatment is expensive and ineffective at altering the course of the cancer, so most owners do not choose aggressive chemotherapy. This puts the life expectancy at one to two months past the original diagnosis, if the pet is lucky to live even that long. Due to the progressive nature of the disease, most pets like Roland are euthanized shortly after diagnosis.

The internal medicine doctor confirmed the unfortunate diagnosis and hopeless prognosis with a cancer specialist, then told Lloyd and Tina that there was really nothing that could be done for their dog. Because there was no specific therapy for his disease, the specialist placed Roland on an analgesic (pain-relieving) medication called butorphanol to make him comfortable, plus the antibiotics amoxicillin and enrofloxacin to help control his fever. At this point Roland's owners contacted me to see if there was any hope for this very hopeless case.

I was confident that ever since Roland began acting ill the case had been handled properly by the medical doctors involved. All of the proper testing had been done by doctors I trusted, several of whom I also use for second opinions on tough cases. The microscopic examination of the aspirates done on Roland's skin tumors confirmed that he did indeed have this horrible disease, so very common in his breed but, thankfully, rarely seen in other breeds.

As I explained to Lloyd and Tina, malignant histiocytosis is a disorder that arises from cells of the immune system. The condition occurs more commonly in the males of this breed, caused by a genetic component that predisposes the pet to develop cancer of a specific cell type in the immune system. Clinical signs that may be seen in other breeds with malignant histiocytosis are similar to those that were affecting Roland, and they include weight loss, lethargy, fever, lymph node enlargement, coughing, and tumor development. The condition is easily diagnosed by microscopic examination of the skin tumors.

Whenever I have to explain to a family that a pet has an untreatable condition, I know I'm delivering very bad news. While Lloyd and Tina had heard the grim prognosis from their other doctors, I knew they wanted a different answer from me. Owners seek help from holistic doctors because they hope that we can offer something, *anything*, that no other doctor can offer. Often our reputations for curing incurable problems and helping patients that no one else can help build up our image (maybe even unrealistically) in the minds of pet owners. While it's true that very often holistic doctors can do some pretty impressive, at times even miraculous, things thanks to all of the therapies we have at our disposal, I have to be honest and realistic with people seeking my help. To say that it's almost impossible to help a pet with such a horrible disease, with a death sentence for a prognosis, especially when no conventional therapy exists, is an understatement. While I always strive to offer hope, that hope can never be false hope.

Consequently, I had the grim task of reconfirming all that had been told to Lloyd and Tina by their other doctors. I honestly told them that I had never had the opportunity to treat malignant histiocytosis, as Roland's breed and his disease are rare and not commonly encountered in most veterinary practices, and I knew that this would be my toughest case to date. I mean, I had a dog with a confirmed fatal disease for which there was no reported conventional treatment, and I couldn't even find any reported natural therapies in the literature to help with his condition, which didn't make me too confident about helping poor Roland! However, we had to try something for him and hope for the best. As I often do with these types of untreatable cases, I made the holistic decision to *treat Roland* rather than try to *treat a disease* for which there exists no treatment.

I started at the beginning and reviewed Roland's diet. No matter what else I do, or what types of therapies I select for my patients, choosing the right diet is critical. Every pet needs to eat, and if we put bad stuff into the body we certainly can't expect healing to occur when the diet is damaging the patient's cells. If the pet is eating bad food, full of potentially harmful by-products and chemicals, filled with low-quality protein, carbohydrates, and rancid fats, which are common to most commercial pet foods, no amount of drugs or supplements can overcome this. Simply put, healing starts with eating the proper food.

Since Tina and Lloyd were very sensitive to their own needs to prepare and eat the best, most organic foods possible, they were already feeding Roland in a similar fashion. His home-made diet consisted of organic raw, or sometimes cooked, high-quality animal proteins. They alternated between buffalo, ostrich, and venison obtained locally from an organic grocery store. Organic vegetables, fruits, and grains rounded out the balance of his meals. They also gave him several high-quality supplements, including kefir and acidophilus. After reviewing Roland's diet, I secretly wished I lived with Lloyd and Tina and had them cook for me!

Many conventional veterinarians don't look too kindly on owners who choose to prepare food for their pets, no doubt due to the strong influences of some of the well-known pet food companies who discourage people from cooking for their pets. I am well aware that there are several valid concerns when owners choose to do so. If they don't follow a proper recipe and use high-quality supplements, it's likely the pet's diet might contain too much or too little of necessary nutrients. Food that is not properly han-dled, especially if offered raw, can easily transmit bacterial and parasitic infections to the pets. In my experience, however, when owners follow a well-balanced recipe, coupled with high-quality supplementation, most pets do very well on homemade diets.

We also discussed vaccines. No pet needs annual vaccina-tions, and fortunately, Lloyd and Tina knew this and had not been vaccinating Roland for several years. They quickly agreed with me that Roland should *never* get another vaccination, as I didn't want to further stress his already taxed immune system and make his disease progress any faster than I feared it would on its own. Since vaccines can bring cancer out of remission, I never vaccinate my cancer patients. While it is true that some pets may require vaccines based upon titer testing, the risk of a cancer patient being exposed to a fatal infectious disease like distemper or parvovirus is so slim that I don't believe it's worth the risk to their health to vaccinate them when they are in remission from their cancer.

I also instructed them not to use any chemicals for flea and tick control. While these chemicals are much safer today than those we used even ten years ago, they are still potent nerve toxins that most pets do not need. Since most pets neither suffer from nor have regular exposure to these external parasites, it makes no sense for most owners to waste their money or to give them to pets that don't need them. And when you consider that these products last in the pet's body for extended periods until they slowly leave the body, I really don't want my patients, especially those suffering from serious diseases, to have them in their bodies. This was welcome news to Lloyd and Tina. They had never used these products on Roland, and did not intend to, as both of them suffered from chemical sensitivities and didn't want to be exposed to these toxins, either.

I knew I would have to get very aggressive with supplementation if Roland was to have any hope of living more than the expected one to two months that he was given by his previous doctors. My goal was to boost his immune system and support his thyroid and adrenal glands (which showed some problems based upon blood testing and which would be very important in keeping Roland's immune system functioning normally).

I began by prescribing two of my favorite immune-supporting formulas at that time, Immuno Support by Rx Vitamins *for* Pets and Immune+, a Chinese herbal formula by Evergreen Herbs. In combination, these two supplements are powerful and have helped me prolong the lives of many cancer patients. Rx Vitamins *for* Pets has now come out with an even stronger formula called ONCO Support, but at the time the Immuno Support was their best product (and continues to be a great supplement to help pets with infectious diseases).

NutriGest by Rx Vitamins *for* Pets was used to support Roland's GI system, as it is the largest part of the immune system and a common source of toxins that find their way into the body. Since Roland had taken conventional medications that were prescribed by his original veterinarian, I knew that his gastrointestinal system had probably received some damage. Hepato Support, another Rx Vitamin *for* Pets product, supports the liver as it attempts to rid the body of cancer cells and their toxic by-products.

A natural adrenal glandular supplement, an antioxidant, and green food were also added to minimize oxidation and inhibit the growth and spread of Roland's aggressive cancer.

Whole-body detoxification is very important for every pet as it enables healing and removes toxins, and there was no question that Roland was quite toxic. A mild detoxification by Heel called Detox-Kit, easily mixed in Roland's water, was prescribed to further rid his body of harmful toxins.

Roland was also prescribed thyroid medication and natural hydrocortisone to be taken as needed, based upon the blood tests performed by his original veterinarian. These would provide continuing support for his weakened thyroid and adrenal glands. While not directly related to his histiocytosis, his abnormal thyroid and adrenal gland values on his recent blood testing required treatment. An important part of an integrative approach to healing pets is to address all of the pet's issues, and not just focus on the present problem. This way, we set the stage for true healing. If only the original problem is dealt with, the pet may never heal, and that secondary problem can block healing and may become a more serious issue in the future.

Lloyd and Tina were very motivated to do anything to help their special friend, and Roland was a great patient and a joy to treat. Since they also lived a very organic lifestyle they wanted to pursue as many natural therapies as possible for Roland. The protocol I designed to help heal him as he fought this horrible disease was readily accepted by all three. Money was not an object for Lloyd and Tina as it is for some pet owners. Since treatment for cases like this can often run into the thousands of dollars, I encourage all of my clients who might not be able to afford this level of care to seriously consider purchasing inexpensive pet health insurance. I never want the cost of care to get in the way of a pet getting the best possible care. It's truly upsetting to know that a pet that could be helped might not receive the required care because the owner can't afford the care. I'm lucky that this is rarely the case in my practice. My clients are strongly bonded with their pets and are usually able to afford to do everything possible to give them the chance to heal. For my part, I do my best to spend their health-care dollars wisely and only when absolutely necessary, setting up a win-win-win situation for the owner, the pet, and me.

I didn't hear from Tina and Lloyd for almost a month following their initial consultation, which is not a good sign when you know the pet you're trying to help heal only has a prognosis of one or two months to live. I left them a message on their answering machine three weeks after I first saw Roland, asking them to call me and let me know how things were going with Roland.

They returned my call a few days later with unexpected but certainly welcome great news. Roland was feeling better! He was no longer lethargic, he seemed more interested in eating and interacting with his owners, his fever had subsided, his tumors were gone, and his abdominal pain had dissipated. He was actually acting normally, just as he had before becoming ill with histiocytosis.

To say I was as thrilled with Roland's progress as his owners were is an understatement. With my experience treating terminal diseases I knew that sometimes a pet would feel better with holistic therapies for a short time, rallying for one final push before the disease would ultimately cause the death of the pet. Still, good news is good news, and I was not one to be pessimistic during the phone call. I did explain that it was possible that this was Roland's last brief rally before succumbing to his malignant histiocytosis. They understood completely, saying that even if his improvement was short-lived they would still be happy with a response no one had predicted or even suggested was possible. I instructed them to continue feeding Roland his great homemade diet, continue his supplement regimen, and of course make sure that he received no vaccinations. I told them to call me if there were any problems, and that I or someone from my office would contact them again in a few weeks to check on Roland's progress.

Roland was first diagnosed with his "fatal" disease over three years ago! As of this writing he is doing well, remains free of malignant histiocytosis, and has had no other health problems. Lloyd and Tina continue to be passionate about their own natural health care as well as Roland's. They are thrilled with the response this special dog has shown, defeating all odds that gave him at most one or two months of poor-quality life following his tragic diagnosis. His supplement regimen remains the same, as he has done well with it. Skeptics might say that this case is simply luck. Well, if that's true then Roland is a lucky boy indeed. In fact, to my knowledge he is the *only* dog in the entire world to be lucky enough to survive this unsurvivable disease, one with a 100 percent mortality rate. Skeptics might also suggest that Roland did not in fact have malignant histiocytosis and was misdiagnosed, which would mean he really didn't survive a fatal disease because he never had it. If this is true, then five veterinarians, three of whom are specialists in their respective fields of internal medicine, oncology, and pathology, were all wrong. I seriously doubt there was any misdiagnosis in this case.

Skeptics might also frown upon my offer of hope for what appeared to be such a hopeless case, and suggest I was only in it to make money by offering false hope for owners who were desperate to hear anything positive about their pet's condition. Those skeptics, however, should keep in mind that I also did not believe there was any treatment that would help Roland. I was as stunned as Lloyd and Tina were to see that Roland was actually healing himself from his fatal condition.

Roland's owners, and millions like them, want to hear some

option that might offer anything positive for their pets, and refuse to give up when health-care providers tell them all seems hopeless. Instead, they want to take a chance on healing, to explore the wonderful but often difficult and sometimes painful journey to better health. They should be given that chance if one exists, no matter how slight. In my opinion, to not try everything possible for every case, no matter how hopeless, is malpractice.

Regardless of the feeble attempts by skeptics to explain away the unexplainable, the reality is that Roland was diagnosed by five veterinarians to have a fatal disease with no known cure. Rather than follow the advice of four of those veterinarians who suggested keeping him comfortable for a few days or weeks until he either passed on his own or needed to be euthanized to end his suffering, Lloyd and Tina chose another option. Familiar with natural therapies based upon their own health needs, they chose something else for Roland, a pathway unfortunately not promoted by many health caregivers or sought by nearly enough pet owners. As Robert Frost so eloquently put it, Lloyd and Tina chose the road "less traveled by, and that has made all the difference" for Roland.

Unexpected miracle. Coincidence. Luck. Misdiagnosis. True healing. Readers are left to ponder what really happened to Roland, but no one can explain away Roland's response to integrative medicine. Like so many of my patients given up for dead by conventional medicine, he is fortunately still with us, thriving rather than simply surviving. But he is a survivor, one of many whose own body used its natural healing energy, augmented by a rational, common-sense approach to healing. While some may choose to dismiss the success in this case, Roland's owners, along with millions of others who understand (as best as any of us are able to understand) true "healing," accept that something quite wonderful, and possibly even miraculous, happened to a very special dog with truly devoted and loving guardians. Long live Roland!

7

Not Hopeless but Needing Hope

It is extremely rewarding indeed when I can help a pet that no one else can help, a pet given up for dead simply because conventional medicine couldn't help and another option was not pursued. I do enjoy helping these special pets, but sometimes a case isn't totally hopeless. Every day I see many cases that while technically not hopeless, still need the help of an integrative doctor.

For these non-life-threatening cases, the owner simply seeks a better treatment than the one proposed by the conventional veterinarian. Maybe that kind of treatment is too expensive, will take too long to work, or is too toxic. If conventional drugs are involved in the originally proposed treatment, the owner may fear the side effects commonly seen with many medications, including secondary diseases that can occur with long-term use of conventional medicines. Regardless of the reason, using an integrative approach is often preferred and better for the owner and pet.

This was the situation with one of my cases where the owner wanted to pursue another of my five goals for holistic care, Goal #2: Say no to drugs for pets unless absolutely necessary.

Boomer

Boomer was a sweet, extremely active yellow Labrador retriever. Like the majority of Labs I see at my practice in Texas, Boomer had skin allergies. Additionally, he was plagued by chronic secondary skin infections with staphylococcal bacteria. His owner, Josh, told me a medical history I've heard thousands of times before from many other pet owners. Boomer started itching when he was about eight months old. His first doctor treated him for allergies with steroids, and Boomer got better quickly, but just as quickly relapsed within a few weeks of running out of his steroid medication. So the doctor gave him more steroids, which helped Boomer again for a few weeks until the medication was stopped, and the itching came back.

After several months of this cycle, Josh sought a second opinion with another local veterinarian, who agreed with the original diagnosis of allergies. Not wanting to commit Boomer to a life sentence of steroids, the second doctor prescribed various antihistamines over the course of several months to see if these would help control Boomer's itching. No surprise: none of the antihistamines provided much relief, although one antihistamine did make him very lethargic. Wanting to help relieve the itching, the second veterinarian had to resort to prescribing more steroids to help Boomer. At this time Boomer also experienced the first of many skin infections, secondary to the allergies, resulting in the chronic use of steroids, and was now placed on an antibiotic, the first of several over the course of the next eight months. While chronic steroid usage is necessary in some people and pets with very serious disorders of the immune system, it can predispose them to chronic infections. This is one of many reasons why steroids should not be used chronically for problems like skin diseases such as allergies unless other therapies are not available.

Finally, a very frustrated Josh and a very itchy Boomer decided to consult a veterinary dermatologist as a last-ditch effort. Numerous tests were done to rule out diseases that commonly masquerade as allergies, including mange, ringworm, food intolerance, and hypothyroidism. Boomer had none of these, and after all the testing and the spending of a lot of money the dermatologist concluded that Boomer suffered from atopy, or allergic dermatitis. To help control Boomer's itching, the dermatologist recommended lifelong antigen therapy (often incorrectly referred to as "allergy shots" by pet owners), which would force Josh to give Boomer injections every one to two weeks to control his itching.

By this time Boomer had been treated for more than two years with multiple drugs. The steroids and antibiotics did help, but Josh realized that Boomer would not be around long if he was always taking steroids and antibiotics. He also did not want to give Boomer shots every week for the rest of his life, and upon hearing that antigen therapy can take up to one year to work, and only really helps control itching in about 60 to 70 percent of allergic dogs, Josh said, "Enough!" At this point he wanted something more than drugs for Boomer and sought my advice.

As is typical of most of my retriever patients, it took longer to greet a very enthusiastic seventy-five-pound Boomer than it did to say hello to Josh. It actually took a few minutes of giving Boomer some of the attention he demanded before I could even make it across the room to shake Josh's hand and welcome him to our practice!

Josh made his intentions very clear from the beginning of the visit. While he appreciated all that Boomer's prior doctors did for him, he knew that administering medications to Boomer was simply a Band-Aid approach, not designed to keep him healthy even if the medications temporarily made Boomer feel better and resolved his skin infections.

My examination of Boomer revealed several physical attributes commonly seen in my patients with skin disease. At first glance Boomer's skin and hair looked normal from my vantage point across the room. When Josh finally got Boomer to lie down and relax, his skin lesions became more apparent. They were typical of lesions seen in dogs with staphylococcal bacterial infections, including pustules (pimples) and scabs on his abdomen and groin. Additionally, Boomer had a slight odor, often noticed in pets with skin infections, and a mild greasiness to his haircoat.

Having seen thousands of allergic pets with secondary skin infections in my practice, I knew that I could do a lot to help Boomer. I explained to Josh that while drug therapy may be necessary on occasion, most of the time Boomer could stay healthy simply by using a few nutritional supplements. Josh agreed that this was what he wanted, and understood that short-term use of medications would be very safe and only prescribed when absolutely needed.

Because Boomer was just starting to break out with yet another infection, both Josh and I judged his skin's current condition to be mild at best and moderate at worst. Therefore, I wanted to try to help his skin heal without using any more antibiotics. Boomer had just finished his latest round of antibiotics about three to four weeks prior to this visit, and his system didn't need any more of these potent medications at this time. Josh agreed that he wanted to get away from using antibiotics, and as I explained, we could always use them again if needed.

To avoid the need for antibiotics, I knew I would have to formulate a pretty aggressive treatment protocol for Boomer. Based upon years of experience helping pets like him, I knew that we couldn't dillydally around and be timid with his treatment if we wanted to avoid medications. With that in mind, here's what I prescribed to help heal Boomer.

First, frequent bathing is *critical* for treating pets with skin disease. The more frequently the pet is bathed, the less likely drugs will be needed as part of the therapy, and when drugs are needed, we can use them for a shorter time when frequent bathing is included in our treatment program. I prescribed a benzoyl peroxide shampoo called Pyoben from Virbac for Boomer. Josh asked if he could use a "people" product. I told him not to do that as the products formulated for people are too strong and would burn Boomer's skin. The Pyoben shampoo would kill the bacteria causing Boomer's staph infection, remove any superficial greasiness on his skin, and reduce the odor caused by his infection. I asked Josh if he felt he could bathe Boomer every day for the first two weeks of his treatment, then reduce the frequency to every two to three days for another two weeks. Even though Boomer was a large, rambunctious dog, Josh was an even bigger guy, and he assured me that while he wasn't looking forward to this frequency of bathing Boomer, he could do it. Since Boomer was a typical Lab that liked water, Josh told me Boomer would enjoy the baths even if *he* didn't necessarily enjoy them that much! When I ask owners of my allergic pets to frequently bathe their animals, I know this is not always easy. I sympathize with them; some pets don't like being bathed, some are too big to easily be put into the bathtub, and some owners have limited time due to job or family commitments. Still, pets with skin disorders that are frequently bathed heal faster and require fewer conventional medicines in order to heal.

Since I didn't think we would need to use traditional antibiotics to help Boomer recover from his staph infection, and since Josh really wanted to avoid all conventional medications if possible, I elected to use two natural products that have replaced antibiotics in most of my skin cases. Oli-Vet is an olive leaf extract manufactured by Vetri-Science that is a wonderful natural antibacterial and antifungal product. I combined this with a great herbal product from Evergreen Herbs called Herbal ABX. Used in combination, this potent therapy has successfully treated most of my pets with all but the most serious staph infections.

In addition to using natural antibacterial herbs and supplements, I typically will help the healing process with supplements designed to boost the pet's immune system to assist in killing the infection. Boomer had suffered for several years from staph infections, and his body had taken a terrible beating from repetitive use of antibiotics and steroids. In short, his immune system was shot and needed help. Therefore, I prescribed Immuno Support, a great herbal supplement from Rx Vitamins, and the homeopathic remedies from Heel, Engystol and Psorinoheel, products that have helped many of my patients with skin disorders of any type, and I felt confident that Boomer would greatly benefit from their use.

Because Boomer had been on antibiotics and steroids for several years, I knew that his gastrointestinal system was also pretty shot. Even short-term use of medications like antibiotics, steroids, and nonsteroidal medications can damage the lining of the intestines. They also kill good, healthy bacteria and yeast that normally reside in the GI tract to keep the GI system functioning normally and to inhibit overgrowth of pathogenic, harmful bacteria. When there is ongoing damage to the intestines a condition called "leaky gut" develops, allowing harmful microorganisms, their toxic by-products, and allergenic proteins to be absorbed into the body. Once this happens, damage can occur anywhere in the patient's body. In Boomer's case, I needed to heal his GI tract to minimize these harmful organisms and toxins from further exacerbating his skin allergies and infections. I prescribed NutriGest from Rx Vitamins *for* Pets and Total Leaky Gut from Nutri-West, two products I've found very helpful in helping pets with any sort of GI damage.

Finally, as I do with all of my patients, I placed Boomer on a high-quality natural diet and told Josh that we would no longer vaccinate Boomer on a regular basis. Instead, we would do annual blood titer testing to determine if and when Boomer needed any vaccines, and only vaccinate him if the titer testing indicated such a need and Boomer's skin was normal at the time.

At his recheck examination one month later, Josh reported that all of Boomer's skin lesions were gone. He tolerated all of his supplements well, and really enjoyed the bathing routine. Josh did ask if he needed to continue with the frequency of the bathing as I had prescribed, as it was quite an effort. Since Boomer's skin looked normal, I wasn't worried about staph infection at that time. Josh told me, however, that Boomer was still itchy, although not nearly as much as when his staph infection was present. To minimize itching and prevent further infections, I asked Josh to bathe Boomer at least one to two times weekly, more if the itching flared up or if the staph lesions returned. Since Boomer was no longer infected, I switched his shampoo to an aloe vera and oatmeal combination, which would cleanse his skin of allergens that caused him to itch as well as reduce inflammation and itching.

The recheck visit is designed to let me know whether my initial diagnosis and treatment were correct. In Boomer's case, he was doing very well! Josh was happy to see his results and even happier to know that Boomer would not need any antibiotics at this time. He also didn't need to continue giving Boomer the antibacterial herbs or the immune-supporting homeopathics.

To prevent frequent future reinfections, I prescribed several products to help Boomer heal for the long haul: the antioxidant called Proanthozone from Animal Health Options and a super-fatty acid product called Ultra EFA from Rx Vitamins *for* Pets. Both of these products reduce inflammation and oxidation, which cause cell damage. Finally, I added my favorite supplement for maintaining a healthy immune system called Vim & Vigor from Pet-Togethers.

Josh was instructed to let me know if signs of infection returned. I felt that if Boomer experienced future infections, we could easily manage them by more frequent bathing with the medicated shampoo and with short-term use of the stronger supplements we used to manage his initial infection.

To date, Boomer has done remarkably well. Each spring and fall, as expected with most of my allergic patients, he does experience a resurgence of his allergies. Occasionally, he starts to get some bumps and scabs on his skin. All of these outbreaks have been easily managed by more frequent bathing, extra supplements for a few weeks, and limited use of low doses of prednisone to control his itching. So far, he has not required any more antibiotics.

Of course, skin disease is not the only condition that I treat with a natural approach. Many other conditions also seem hopeless in the sense that owners see no end in sight except chronic drug therapy. They don't want to continue using medications that fail to improve the pet's condition. In their minds, while certainly not fatal or imminently life-threatening, any chance of recovery seems hopeless to them.

Mr. B

While Boomer's story exemplifies a typical condition I see in dogs, Mr. B's story is very typical of a problem many cat owners experience.

Mr. B., who shared a house with three other cats, two dogs, and his owners, Phil and Monica, was a five-year-old male Ragdoll cat. For those not familiar with this breed, Ragdolls are great cats to have as companions. My own Ragdoll, Dysa, is the first cat I've ever owned (I was always raised with dogs since my mother has been allergic to cats most of her life). These wonderful felines began as a cross between a Persian and a Birman.

They are called Ragdolls because, when picked up and carried, they become limp like rag dolls. I have very fond memories of my daughter Erica and her friends carrying around Dysa in shopping bags, moving her from room to room with nary a peep from her! Ragdolls have a great temperament, being very gentle and loving animals. They are often called people's best companions and are a pleasure to own. If you're not really a cat person but want to tiptoe into the waters of feline companionship, the Ragdoll breed is a great way to start!

Phil and Monica came to see me because of Mr. B.'s chronic and upsetting problem: FLUTD, an acronym for feline lower urinary tract disease (formerly called FUS, or feline urological syndrome), and the most common condition of the urinary tract (mainly the bladder) in cats. It is similar to a condition called idiopathic sterile cystitis in people in that we still don't know the cause of this debilitating feline disorder. There is no similar condition that occurs in dogs. Many theories exist about the cause, but nothing has been proven. What is known is that some cats develop crystals in the urinary bladder that irritate the lining of the bladder, cause inflammation and bleeding. Clinical signs occur as a result of the inflammation and include difficulty going to the bathroom, bloody urine, urinating in inappropriate places outside of the litter box in the home, and blockage of the urethra in male cats.

Mr. B. had experienced several episodes of FLUTD over the past few years. Twice they resulted in blockage of his urethra, making it impossible for him to urinate and requiring emergency care, and costing several hundred dollars per episode to relieve his obstruction. Since there is no known cause for the problem, and since conventional medicine really doesn't offer much to help these pets, Phil and Monica certainly were faced with a "hopeless" situation as far as any cure or long-lasting treatment for Mr. B.

As we began our visit, I could hear the frustration in their voices as they related Mr. B.'s history of illness. They were especially frustrated with their current veterinarian's recommendation that he undergo what they felt was a demeaning and disfiguring surgery to remove his penis as a way to prevent future emergency urethral blockages!

I then began discussing FLUTD. As I explained to them, there is no known cause for this problem, although we do know that some cats will develop FLUTD as a result of stress. Others develop it by eating a certain brand or type of food but do well on other foods. Some cats with FLUTD have no obvious inciting factors. I also told them that their frustration with Mr. B.'s condition was also shared by veterinarians who have a very difficult time treating pets without knowing what causes the condition they are trying to treat.

In reviewing Mr. B.'s records I saw that he had been treated repeatedly with the antibiotic amoxicillin, and twice with the antibiotic Baytril (enrofloxacin.) Amoxicillin is commonly used—and I would argue overused and misused—in both human and veterinary medicine. As I explained that antibiotics have almost no place in the treatment of FLUTD, Phil and Monica told me their prior veterinarian, as well as the emergency-clinic veterinarians who treated Mr. B.'s two obstructive episodes, had referred to his problem as a bladder infection, hence the need for the amoxicillin. I told them that unlike the situation in dogs and people, cats very rarely get actual bladder infections. (I've only seen a few proven culture-positive cases in more than twenty years of practice!)

While I don't have a problem in using antibiotics in cases of severe bloody urination, most cats with FLUTD, like Mr. B., don't need or receive any benefit from antibiotics. When I explained this to Phil and Monica, they told me that Mr. B. did improve after his antibiotic therapy. I informed them that would have happened no matter what was done, as most cats with FLUTD will recover with supportive care within a few days. When they heard this, they were visibly distraught that their poor cat had been treated with so many drugs that really were not necessary and could have harmed him.

Skeptics will also argue that cats recovering from FLUTD after treatment with natural therapies would have otherwise recovered, but they miss two important points. First, wouldn't it make sense to use something natural and without side effects rather than antibiotics if the pet will recover anyway? Additionally, the natural therapies will help the cats recover more quickly and make them feel better as they are recovering and will minimize recurrences.

Second, I'm not as concerned about a quick recovery as I am about preventing future episodes of FLUTD. Giving antibiotics to a pet does nothing to prevent future episodes. Aside from receiving no benefit from this therapy, pets are harmed by it. All drugs have side effects, and we certainly don't need to contribute to the ever growing and dangerous problem of antibiotic resistance. Using natural therapies offers the best chance to minimize if not totally prevent future problems with FLUTD in pets like Mr. B.

I also took the time to address the very distressing suggestion by their veterinarian that Mr. B. undergo surgery to remove his penis. It is true that some male cats do need this drastic but lifesaving procedure. Removing the penis allows the urethra to be enlarged surgically, which will almost totally prevent further blockages by the crystals that cause the signs seen with FLUTD. This surgery can be lifesaving when done properly in carefully selected pets. However, it should not be done except as a last resort, after all the other therapies have been tried without success. Even then, it will not prevent further episodes of FLUTD (we still need to find something to do that) but it will usually prevent future urethral blockages, which are fatal unless immediately treated.

At this visit, I needed to offer something to help Mr. B.'s immediate issue of painful, bloody urination. I also needed to set the stage for lifelong control, so that he would not continue to experience repeated episodes that might ultimately require surgery. As I do with all healing therapies, I began our treatment discussion by talking about diet. I had been taught as a conventional doctor that it really didn't matter if cats with FLUTD were fed dry or canned food. Since becoming a holistic doctor, I knew this "fact" was no longer correct. Cats that eat wet food (a natural canned or homemade diet) do better than cats that eat dry food. The more water that cats with bladder issues receive, the more they urinate, and when cats urinate frequently, they flush the bladder of the crystals and debris that cause FLUTD.

Phil and Monica were currently feeding Mr. B. a dry version of one of the popular prescription-type diets, designed for cats with bladder problems. When I asked why they were feeding Mr. B. dry food rather than canned, they told me that he didn't like the canned version of this food and refused to eat it.

I explained to them why it was important to give cats with FLUTD wet foods. I also shared with them some of the problems with the medicated diet they were feeding Mr. B. First, unless it was the only diet that controlled his problem (which wasn't true or they wouldn't be in my office for his ongoing problem), these types of food are not "natural" and often contain harmful by-products and chemicals. Also, while some of these foods can dissolve crystals and even stones in the bladder, they may predispose the formation of different kinds of crystals and stones. For example, while the diets might reduce the formation of struvite crystals and stones, they can increase the likelihood of the formation of oxalate crystals and stones. Therefore, I tend not to prescribe these medicated diets.

Instead, I suggested either a great canned food made by one of the several natural-food companies I recommend, or a homemade diet if they preferred. Due to their busy schedules, they both agreed that preparing food at home was out of the question. Since Mr. B. had eaten several brands of canned food in the past, they were certain he would enjoy a canned natural food and would switch him to one.

I also prescribed supplements I've used in many of my FLUTD patients that I've found quite successful to help Mr. B. The first is called UT Strength by Vetri-Science, a great herbal preparation for any pet with diseases of the urinary system. Best of all, it's a chewable treat, so I knew Mr. B. was likely to enjoy taking it. Second was a homeopathic remedy called Uri-Cleanse from Heel. Along with this, because Mr. B. had experienced so many episodes of his FLUTD, I prescribed the homeopathic remedy cantharis to use for two weeks.

I also included my old standby Vim & Vigor from Pet-Togethers plus the antioxidant Proanthozone from Animal Health Options. These would help Mr. B. stay healthy after he recovered from his latest bout with FLUTD.

Phil and Monica were happy to try this approach, and even happier to hear that I was not going to send them home with antibiotics or steroids. After I explained that the remedies I prescribed were easy to administer to cats, they felt they would have no problem giving them to Mr. B. I asked them to give me an update in one week so we could adjust our treatment if things didn't progress as I expected.

One week later I talked with a very excited Monica who reported that Mr. B. was doing great! He was taking his supplements well, really enjoyed his UT Strength "treat," and had not experienced any more recurrences of FLUTD. They also found several flavors of natural canned foods that Mr. B. really liked. I told her to continue the supplements until they were gone, and to get refills for the UT Strength, Vim & Vigor, and Proanthozone as I wanted him to stay on these supplements indefinitely to keep him healthy and to reduce further occurrences of FLUTD.

These are just two of the many types of disorders that can

benefit pets from a holistic perspective in health care. Many owners can now choose another path to end their pets' pain, suffering, and disease. All it takes is a strong desire for them to say *no* to drugs, find someone who can offer something different and more natural for the pet, maintain an open mind, and work with the pet to help it heal itself. The health-care crisis in human medicine also extends to pet medicine. By focusing on healing and prevention for chronic problems, people who are interested in true health discover the miracles all around them in the form of integrative, natural, holistic health care.

8

Second Opinions...

It's Not Hopeless, It Just Seems That Way!

Holistic veterinarians like myself are consulted by pet owners for a variety of reasons. They might be seeking a holistic approach to treating a specific problem, or the pet's condition might have been labeled hopeless by conventional doctors and specialists. Over the years that I have been practicing integrative medicine, however, I've noticed that many pet owners come to see me because they want something else, such as a second opinion on a pet's case, or maybe an answer to a question a prior veterinarian was unable to answer.

Some of these owners take a more natural approach to their own care and are seeking something similar for their pets. Others are upset that conventional care has not solved their pets' problems. Many owners are spending large amounts of money on pet care and not seeing an end in sight, and want to find a way to cut their costs. This makes good sense, as a natural approach to maintaining pet health usually costs less than treating a pet that is always sick, requiring multiple visits to the doctor and many medications.

Sometimes the pets actually are worse off on the conventional treatments, and a second disease occurs as a result of the therapy. For example, pets taking steroids often gain weight, eat a lot, drink a lot of water, and therefore urinate a lot. Some of these pets develop urinary incontinence, diabetes, or chronic infections as a result of the steroid therapy.

Pets on chronic antibiotic therapy may develop more severe, secondary infections with more pathogenic bacteria and yeasts. Dogs and cats taking medications for heart disease may become weak, lethargic, and show a decreased appetite. Pets with inflammatory bowel disease, bladder disease, skin disease, or seizures often develop side effects and secondary diseases from their chronic therapies.

When I started practicing integrative medicine many years ago, I never expected to serve as a source for a second opinion for a pet's original diagnosis. Nor did I expect to discover something very disturbing—that I would see so many pets with an incorrect diagnosis! I continue to be amazed that many pets are originally diagnosed with terrible diseases and given hopeless prognoses, even though the pets do not have the diagnosed diseases. Many pets that I see have been given up on by the original doctor, yet have nothing seriously wrong with them. Thankfully, their owners were disbelieving when the original doctor made a diagnosis that indicated a serious problem in an otherwise fairly healthy and normal pet! Here are a few of my memorable cases where a second opinion was lifesaving.

Bailey

Bailey was a middle-aged, very friendly tricolor beagle. His appearance and happy-go-lucky attitude reminded me of Spotty, my first dog, also a male tricolored beagle, who was my special companion from the time I was eight years old. I was happy to see, upon entering the examination room to meet Bailey and his human parents, Debbie and Rick, that Bailey looked quite well. His medical record listed his diagnosis as kidney failure, but he looked awfully good for a dog with such a dismal diagnosis.

Bailey's owners, who outwardly seemed very happy to be at our office, began the conversation by relating to me a very sad and troubling story indeed. Bailey had just been diagnosed with kidney failure the preceding Friday morning, a few days prior to this visit. Apparently he had not been feeling well for a few days, prompting the visit to their regular veterinarian. After drawing blood for a comprehensive blood count and blood profile, several of Bailey's kidney enzymes came back elevated above the normal range. Specifically, two tests that commonly screen for kidney problems, his Blood Urea Nitrogen, BUN, and creatinine, were elevated. Based upon these findings Bailey's veterinarian diagnosed terminal kidney failure, and painted a very grim picture for him.

Depending upon the stage of kidney failure, it can be a very serious diagnosis (if diagnosed late in the disease) or a more be-nign one (if caught very early before permanent damage is done to the kidneys). However, from what Debbie and Rick shared with me, his prior veterinarian painted a very hopeless picture for their special friend.

I asked Debbie and Rick how Bailey was feeling since their visit to that vet a few days before. They both told me that he was feeling better. He never had been very sick, only a little under the weather with a reduced appetite for a few days, which caused them to be skeptical of the veterinarian's hopeless prognosis.

The diagnosis and prognosis given by Bailey's veterinarian didn't really make sense to me. If Bailey was dying of kidney fail-ure, he should be deathly ill. Instead I was petting a very happy and definitely healthy-looking beagle.

I asked Debbie and Rick what type of therapy their veterinar-ian had given Bailey for his kidney failure. They replied that nothing had been recommended, as the veterinarian told them that kidney failure is fatal and to take Bailey home, enjoy a final few days with him over the weekend, and return on Monday morning for euthanasia to relieve his suffering. Heartbroken, upset with such a final and dismal prognosis, but also troubled that the doctor offered no help at all for Bailey, who they could see was not acting like he was near death, they left the doctor's office and drove home, not sure what to do next. They had a fit-ful weekend, wondering what would happen to Bailey. One thing they knew for certain was that there was no way they were going back to their veterinarian to have Bailey euthanized. They had had pets their entire lives, and did actually have to make the decision for euthanasia in the past, but those decisions were made knowing that their pets were suffering and failing to respond to the prescribed therapies. Bailey was just too healthy to be that sick, and euthanasia was not a decision they were ready to make.

I was very upset upon hearing their story. Bailey's kidney enzymes did not support a diagnosis of end-stage, fatal kidney failure. As I reviewed his medical record, I noticed that other laboratory tests were normal, those that should have been abnormal if kidney failure was present. His phosphorus, red blood cell count, and urinalysis were all normal. As I suspected, Bailey was not in fact dying of kidney failure, and euthanasia was definitely not an option! While this was certainly good news for Bailey, it was not necessarily good news for my profession. Once again the all-too-common practice of misdiagnosis and the sentencing to death of a pet that was not seriously ill had reared its ugly head. Deep down inside I know that we all make mistakes, but in my opinion this was not a simple mistake but rather a gross misdiagnosis that elevated itself to the level of malpractice. I shudder when I think how many pets like Bailey have their lives prematurely ended due to a similar medical error. While it is estimated that 5 to 10 percent of human patients die from medical errors (misdiagnoses, infections picked up while hospitalized, side effects from conventional medications, etc.), no one knows how many pets suffer the same tragic fate, but based upon what I see every day in my practice I'm sure it is at least that amount.

I shared the good news with Debbie and Rick. While Bailey had a very slight elevation in some of his kidney enzymes, at worst he had very early mild kidney disease. I explained to his owners, now ecstatic at the news that Bailey was not dying, that they caught a potentially serious and even fatal problem very early. At this stage of his disease there were many things we could offer him that conventional medicine could not.

As I shared with Debbie and Rick, conventional medicine is wonderful when used appropriately and can help many pets, but it can't help pets who do not have a disease. Bailey seemed to have early kidney disease but not yet kidney failure. Conventional medicine can't treat kidney disease at this early stage as at that point it doesn't offer anything for otherwise healthy pets. This is a large gray area where the pet isn't normal, but isn't afflicted with something serious, so it really can't be treated since the pet doesn't yet have a disease.

This is a great time, though, for an integrative approach using natural therapies. Natural medicine intervenes at this early stage, helping slightly damaged organs *before* they fail and a name is given to the disease. At this stage of early diagnosis, natural medicine works wonders to keep pets alive and to prolong or even prevent a disease from forming.

Debbie and Rick were so happy to know that their decision to seek a second opinion was correct. My diagnosis and very positive prognosis confirmed their decision to avoid euthanasia and seek help for their special friend. They were very interested in pursuing any therapies that would help Bailey live as long as possible and restore his health.

For Bailey, I prescribed several natural therapies to help heal his slightly injured kidneys, supporting them and keeping them healthy as long as possible, in an effort to prevent kidney failure.

I prescribed a fish oil supplement high in omega-3 fatty acids. The EPA and DHA omega-3s can reduce inflammation in the body and are one of my standard supplements for pets with any condition, as inflammation accompanies cell and organ damage.

Since Bailey was already eating a high-quality natural diet, I advised Debbie and Rick to continue with that food. At this early stage of kidney disease some doctors advocate medicated diets to minimize excessive amounts of harmful proteins entering the blood. However, I have not seen a need to do this if the pet is already eating a quality diet. I prefer to reserve medicated diets for pets that absolutely need them, as they are not natural and usually contain by-products and chemicals that I feel do further damage to compromised organs.

I also used a homeopathic product called Heel Kidney, designed to assist in the healing of any damage to these organs. With these two supplements and his good diet I felt that Bailey did not need any other specific care at this time. I told Debbie and Rick that while these therapies would help Bailey, his kidney disease would likely progress to kidney failure at some point. For now, there was no reason to worry, as Bailey was doing well and should continue to stay healthy for quite some time.

Debbie and Rick left with Bailey, armed with the treatments that would help him live a healthy lifestyle, and comforted in knowing they had made the right decision, a decision that saved Bailey from an unnecessary and untimely death.

Over the years I had the opportunity to carefully monitor Bailey's health with frequent examinations and blood and urine testing. He did develop a pretty bad bout of liver disease, which we successfully treated with natural therapies, but his kidneys were not harmed and he continued to remain happy and healthy, providing Debbie and Rick with many wonderful adventures and memories.

Four years after his original misdiagnosis of fatal kidney failure, Bailey's kidney disease did finally develop into true kidney failure. At this point we changed his diet to a canned version of a medicated food. In an attempt to keep kidney patients very well hydrated, most holistic doctors prefer moist food with their higher water content.

At this time it was also necessary that I alter his supplement regimen. In addition to his fatty acids and homeopathic therapy, I added the antioxidant Proanthozone from Animal Health Options, UT Strength from Vetri-Science, Whole System Kidney, a balanced glandular and herbal product from Nutri-West, and a special Chinese herbal mixture called Kidney Formula specially made for my practice.

I also taught Debbie and Rick how to administer fluids under Bailey's skin at home each day. This fluid therapy, easily administered by their owners, is a life-saving therapy for many pets. Administering fluids at home is often the difference between life and death as the kidneys start to degenerate, and I have kept many pets alive for many years simply by adding fluid therapy to the treatment regimen. While not as helpful as true dialysis, which is neither practical for most pets nor affordable for most owners, this "diruesis" therapy is critical in reducing the harmful toxins that build up in the blood as a pet's kidneys fail. Bailey, being a very gentle patient, sat patiently on our treatment table as my technician demonstrated the procedure to Debbie and Rick. They were eager to do anything to keep Bailey a part of their family as long as possible, and easily learned how to gently insert the needle under Bailey's skin in order to give him the fluid therapy he needed. They were now intimately involved in Bailey's care, and this extra level of involvement further increased the special bond between them.

With this new, more intensive regimen of holistic therapies, and the dedication and love of his owners, Bailey pulled through his episode of kidney failure and did very well for the next twelve months. Follow-up visits to our office during this time showed that while his kidneys would never again return to normal, his kidney failure had stabilized and was well controlled. While Debbie and Rick delighted each time I gave them the good news after receiving the results from Bailey's blood and urine testing, they knew deep down that eventually the news would not be so good. For now, though, they continued to love Bailey each day, and he returned their love with his usual happy greeting when they made it home from work.

While Bailey hung on as long as he could without a kidney transplant, which is beyond the abilities of most owners, his kidneys continued to fail despite his therapy. One year after beginning his daily fluid therapy, Bailey's kidneys did fail for the last time. Despite hospitalization and intensive treatment with intravenous fluids and antibiotics for seventy-two hours, he failed to respond. The sad look in his tired eyes as we finished his last treatment told all of us that it was time to say good-bye. He had fought a valiant fight, and had lived an extra few years, thanks to the determination of his loving owners. We all agreed that the final gift of love we could give Bailey was to end the terrible suffering that accompanies kidney failure, as uremic toxins accumulated in his body and began shutting down all of his organs. Debbie and Rick gently wept, tenderly petting Bailey's head, as I administered the overdose of intravenous anesthetic that would quickly end Bailey's suffering and send him to a better place. Bailey looked lovingly into their eyes, gave one final sigh, and quickly passed.

A few weeks following his passing, I received a lovely note of appreciation from Rick and Debbie, thanking me for giving Bailey every chance possible, and for helping keep him healthy during the time I was his caregiver. They were especially thankful that they had another five years with their special friend, time they would have never had if they had done his euthanasia at the time of his mistaken diagnosis of fatal kidney failure. Their dedication to Bailey the beagle was obvious while they cared for him. The love they have for this breed is evident today as they serve as foster parents for other beagles who are looking for permanent homes as loving as the one provided by Debbie and Rick.

While Bailey was typical of many of the pets I see who do not have nearly as serious a problem as the initial misdiagnosis suggests, occasionally I see pets who really are very sick. Their owners also want a second opinion to confirm or deny that initial opinion.

Little Bit

Little Bit was another older pet I saw who was diagnosed with kidney failure. Pat and Sandy, his loving owners, didn't want to accept the death sentence imposed by his regular veterinarian who offered no hope upon seeing his blood testing. Hoping I might be able to offer something to help Little Bit, they sought my opinion.

Little Bit was very special to Pat and Sandy, a retired couple who doted on this obviously spoiled mixed-breed dog who had just turned fifteen years old. Pat, who wore a World War II cap, had served in the military. He told me that he had been in the coast guard during the war, and was stationed in the South Pacific. I shared with him that my father had also served in that branch of the military, and had a few tours in the South Pacific area as well. He was now retired from his work in the banking industry. He and Sandy, a housewife and mother, had raised many pets while their three children were growing up. Since all of their children now had families of their own, they devoted all of their time and attention to their grandchildren and to Little Bit.

As they shared stories of Little Bit with me, I appreciated how attached they really were to this small dog. While they loved their children and their grandchildren, Little Bit lived with them twenty-four hours each day and was their constant companion. In effect, he was their new child.

I appreciated their love and concern for their furry friend. Pat and Sandy did not want to accept that the end was near for Little Bit. While many owners do not want to accept reality, or at least are not properly prepared for a dismal diagnosis and prognosis, Pat and Sandy had a very legitimate reason for questioning the original opinion. Little Bit looked and acted totally normal, in no way resembling the typical pet dying of kidney failure.

Dogs and cats in this situation literally look like they are close to death, and many really are. These poor creatures have stopped eating and are very depressed and lethargic as uremic toxins build up in the body, rather than being filtered and excreted in the urine by normally functioning kidneys. But Little Bit looked like a normal older dog, wagging his tail as I approached him on the examination table, even putting his head under my extended right hand as he asked to be scratched and petted on his head.

I did review the medical records with Pat and Sandy, who told me that when Little Bit seemed to be eating less for a few days they had taken him to his doctor a week prior to our visit. The blood testing done that day indicated to his doctor that Little Bit was in end-stage kidney failure. The doctor shared this bad news with Pat and Sandy, and told them Little Bit should be euthanized immediately to prevent the future suffering that would invariably occur as his kidneys gave out.

I looked at the blood tests they brought with them and was quite surprised to see that the original doctor was correct! Little Bit's lab results were among the worst I have seen for pets with kidney failure. I was stunned that this little dog, who was truly dying on the inside, didn't seem to know or care about it because he acted like a totally normal dog.

I had the difficult job of telling Pat and Sandy that the original veterinarian was correct, as Little Bit's laboratory values were not really compatible with life. I did, however, want to offer all of them some hope. Since Little Bit seemed to be feeling relatively normal, there was no way I would recommend euthanasia at that time. Pat and Sandy also indicated that they could never end the life of their special friend while he was still happy and enjoying life with them.

I did tell them that Little Bit really was sick, very sick, and in fact did not have much time left based upon his laboratory testing, but that the holistic approach is about treating pets, not treating lab results. Therefore, as long as patients like Little Bit have the will to live, I have the will to help them live as long and as happily as possible.

I honestly shared with Pat and Sandy that it was unlikely I was going to save their only companion, and that death really could come any day. I told them that I wanted all of us to do whatever it took to give Little Bit as much time as possible to still love them and provide them his wonderful companionship, and that with their help we would take every day they had with Little Bit as a blessing. I did have them promise that when Little Bit's body finally gave out, they would be ready to end his life humanely so he would not suffer. They both assured me that while they wanted Little Bit to live as long as possible, they accepted my opinion that he probably would not be with them much longer and would never let him suffer. With this understanding I prescribed a very aggressive protocol to help Little Bit stay healthy and happy for whatever time he had left with us.

I prescribed a regimen similar to that used for Bailey when his kidneys finally began to fail, including several herbs and homeopathics, a canned medicated diet, and, of course, intensive fluid therapy to be administered at home by Pat and Sandy. While this protocol helped Little Bit for several weeks, his poor kidneys gave out about one month after starting his treatment. As agreed, Pat and Sandy said good-bye to him as I ended his suffering in our office with an overdose of intravenous anesthetic.

Ending a pet's life through the humane act of euthanasia is

never an easy task, even when I know it's the humane, correct thing to do. While my staff and I must always deal with our own emotions, they are rarely as strong as those expressed by the pet's family. Pat and Sandy really loved their special pet. Even though they knew the time had come to end Little Bit's suffering, and had been preparing themselves for this moment for more than a month, they were heartbroken with grief. Pat especially found it difficult to say good-bye to Little Bit. A tough old guy who I'm sure had seen some pretty horrible things during his service to our country in World War II, he found it difficult to hide his true emotions for this special little dog. I hugged both of them and offered them some tissue, reassuring them that while this was a difficult decision on their part, it was nonetheless humane, correct, and a very selfless act. Little Bit was lucky to have had them as owners and was now in a better place. I told them to stay with Little Bit as long as they wanted, and that when they finished saying good-bye to him, we would notify the pet cemetery to come and take him for cremation.

While Little Bit was one of those truly hopeless cases that I see way too late in the course of their diseases, he taught us that hope should still be offered as long as the pet has the will to live. He wasn't ready to give up when first diagnosed, even if his original doctor felt that was the best choice. And since he had truly dedicated owners that wanted to continue loving him as long as he was able to return that love, they were happy to give him another month of a wonderful life until he finally was ready to let go and pass into the next world. For at least the last month of his life, his holistic treatment gave him a few more weeks, and they were a good few weeks.

Misdiagnosis and a second opinion are not simply limited to a misinterpretation of blood values for kidney disease. I commonly see pets misdiagnosed with liver failure that actually have adrenal gland disease.

Fluffy and Furball

One of my favorite families, Cathy and Andy, had several Pomeranian dogs. These furry and fluffy little balls of excitement make great pets, but as a breed they have several problems as they age. Heart disease, bronchitis, and tracheal disease are very common in these dogs. Adrenal gland disease, frequently misdiagnosed as liver disease, is something I see frequently in these great dogs.

I began my Monday afternoon visiting with Cathy and Andy and their two middle-aged Pomeranians, Fluffy and Furball. Fluffy was the older of the two, having just celebrated her ninth birthday. Furball was just a tad younger at seven years old. Cathy and Andy wanted to consult with me about Fluffy's recent diagnosis of liver disease. Since Furball and Fluffy were very attached and went everywhere together, Furball joined the family for this visit.

According to Cathy and Andy, Fluffy had always been a very healthy lady. In reviewing her records, I noticed that her owners took exceptional care of her. She was taken to her veterinarian every year for her annual checkup and vaccinations, and had regular dental cleanings as recommended by the doctor. Since they also brought Furball's medical records with them, I reviewed those, too, noting equally outstanding care for her as well.

I paid particular attention to notations made by the veterinarian over the preceding three months after he had diagnosed Fluffy as having liver disease. During a routine preoperative blood profile for the recommended dental cleaning, the doctor noted an increased value for one of her biochemical tests called alkaline phosphatase (abbreviated SAP or ALP on the laboratory form). Normal values for this test run around 150, and Fluffy's value was slightly over double that at 332. The veterinarian suspected liver disease and placed Fluffy on a two-week course of the antibiotic amoxicillin. His notations indicated he felt that the increased SAP enzymes indicated a bacterial infection of the liver, probably due to normal bacteria in the small intestine traveling up the bile duct and infecting the liver.

During Fluffy's follow-up visit with the veterinarian at the end of her antibiotic treatment, the doctor noted on the medical records that she still did not have any obvious clinical signs. A repeated blood profile showed that the SAP had not decreased and instead had increased to 386. He prescribed another two-week round of antibiotics, this time using a very strong medication called Baytril.

During her next follow-up visit at the end of her Baytril therapy, her SAP was still elevated at a value of 379. At this point, suspecting something very serious with her liver, he recommended surgery to perform a liver biopsy and get to the root of her problem. Upon hearing the recommendation for a surgical biopsy, Cathy and Andy decided they wanted a second opinion and came to see me.

As I reviewed the medical records and listened to their story, I immediately suggested that Fluffy did not in fact have liver disease. Her liver enzymes were actually normal on the various blood testing that had been done. The only clinically significant abnormality was her elevated SAP.

As I explained to Cathy and Andy, the SAP enzyme can elevate due to several different conditions. First, it certainly can increase in pets with liver or gallbladder disease. However, in most of those cases I expect to see elevations in other tests that point toward these organs, including her bilirubin, GGT, ALT, and bile acids. All of these tests were normal, and Fluffy certainly wasn't sick, making liver disease extremely unlikely.

The second and by far the most common reason for an elevated SAP in a middle-aged dog of Fluffy's breed is from an increase in blood cortisol levels. While this can occur in pets given synthetic or natural steroids, by injection or orally, Fluffy had not recently been treated with any steroidal drugs. This meant that her adrenal glands, the normal source of cortisol, were making excessive amounts of this hormone. I suspected that Fluffy's adrenal glands, not her liver, were the cause of her abnormal blood tests. This condition is so common that at least 50 percent of the older dogs I see in my practice have adrenal disease, and it's something I'm always looking for in my older canine patients.

In advanced cases of adrenal disease, the condition is termed Cushing's disease and often requires potent chemotherapy to control the disease. One thing you never want to do to a pet with Cushing's disease is a liver biopsy. A side effect of elevated cortisol levels is decreased wound healing. I saw a case many years ago where the pet was misdiagnosed with having liver disease, and a liver biopsy was performed. It took a very long time for the surgical incision to heal since the actual diagnosis was Cushing's disease. Unfortunately, this poor pet, a middle-aged dachshund (another breed likely to develop adrenal disease), died shortly after my consultation with his owner.

Fortunately for Fluffy, no conventional medical treatment was needed at this time (and has not been needed as of the time I'm writing this book, some six years later). One of the reasons is that conventional medicine actually has nothing to treat adrenal disease until it develops into Cushing's disease. As a result, pets with adrenal disease in which the SAP is elevated are in a gray area. They're not really normal, yet don't have a disease recognized by conventional medicine.

The good news is that an alternative approach works very well for pets in this gray area. The Eastern or holistic approach doesn't require a diagnosis. Rather, the goal is to heal damaged organs using a variety of nutrients, herbs, and homeopathics. True illness is not required for using a holistic approach, only an abnormality somewhere in the body. While Western medicine, which relies on conventional medications, can be helpful in treating acute and life-threatening problems, and can control pain and inflammation when used on a limited as-needed basis for chronic problems, the holistic approach is the better choice for staying healthy and assisting healing from chronic illness. Both approaches have their place in patient care, but for day-to-day health, the holistic approach is preferred, and it is what I, my family, and my clients all embrace with open minds and open hearts.

In talking with Cathy and Andy I let them know that a liver biopsy was not needed and could actually be detrimental. Instead of liver disease, I told them that I thought Fluffy actually had adrenal gland disease. Therefore, the holistic approach was perfect and could do a lot to help her. Cathy and Andy were quite relieved to hear this, and quite happy that they had sought a second opinion before subjecting Fluffy to unnecessary and possibly very dangerous surgery.

The regimen I prescribed for Fluffy utilized herbs to nourish and strengthen the adrenal glands, helping them function normally for as long as possible. I prescribed the adrenal gland supplement called Adreno-Lyph from Nutri-West. This powerful glandular supplement supports and nourishes the adrenal glands, and it is useful for pets with any adrenal gland problems or excess stress. The choline and B-vitamin–containing supplement called Cholodin from MVP Laboratories was also prescribed for Fluffy. It normalizes levels of the major nerve transmitter, acetylcholine, used to minimize cognitive difficulties in older pets. I also find it very helpful in all of my patients with adrenal gland, liver, or pancreatic problems.

Finally, I used an herbal supplement specially made for my practice called Adrenal Gland/Cushing's Formula. This powerful combination of Chinese herbs attempts to nourish the damaged adrenal glands, reduce cortisol levels, and in patients with Cushing's disease, actually function like conventional drugs in reducing clinical signs that often occur with the disease.

Fluffy was very easy to treat, and Cathy and Andy reported no problems in giving her the prescribed treatment. A recheck of her blood one month after starting her holistic therapies showed a lowering of her SAP levels (to 250) and no other problems. I told Cathy and Andy that the holistic approach can help pets with adrenal disease but doesn't always return the blood results to normal. My main goal in treating these special pets is to stabilize, possibly even lower, the abnormal blood results, and of course prevent the development of Cushing's disease, which would eventually happen if nothing were done.

The long-term prognosis for Fluffy and pets like her is really good when treated with a holistic approach. Regular examinations and monitoring of the pet's blood and urine are very important. The supplements are changed or adjusted depending upon the patient's response to them and what happens with the laboratory parameters. In Fluffy's case, monitoring every six months was adequate. Other patients might need to be seen every three to four months depending upon their circumstances.

Because the liver can be secondarily affected in pets with adrenal gland disease, other supplements may also be needed to support the liver.

With only a handful of exceptions, none of my patients with adrenal gland disease that I treated with the holistic approach have gone on to develop true Cushing's disease. Those few pets whose blood testing worsened despite the appropriate supplementation had abdominal ultrasound examinations to look at the adrenal glands, gall bladder, and liver. These pets unfortunately developed adrenal gland cancer, which caused their blood values to worsen. The holistic approach to treating adrenal gland disease is so successful in preventing pets from developing Cushing's disease that I always suspect adrenal cancer in any pet that worsens on my supplement therapy.

Fluffy did very well and has not developed any liver problems or Cushing's disease. Furball also developed adrenal gland disease a few years after I first met her. Like with Fluffy, prescribing herbs and nutritional supplements stabilized Furball's condition and she also has not developed liver disease or adrenal cancer.

When I first began exploring alternative medicine, I started with nutrition, then quickly moved on to learning about herbs and homeopathics. Soon I found myself interested in acupuncture, one of the oldest forms of alternative medicine. I chose to learn about acupuncture for two reasons. First, it is the most well-known alternative therapy, and owners constantly asked me to offer it to their pets. Second, I saw (and still do see) many patients with orthopedic (musculoskeletal) disorders. Acupuncture often works well for patients with joint and back problems, so I knew that by learning this technique I would have no shortage of patients I could help. Learning acupuncture allowed me to provide an additional therapy that would prove useful for many of my patients.

By far the most common musculoskeletal disorder I see in my practice involves joint diseases of primarily middle-aged to older, larger breeds of dogs. The most common disease I see in these patients is hip dysplasia, and many owners come to me with that diagnosis for their dogs, hoping that acupuncture or some other alternative therapy might help.

Hip dysplasia is a common disease of many larger breeds of dogs. The condition can be seen in any dog or cat but typically affects retrievers, German shepherds, rottweilers, mastiffs, and Dobermans. It can occur in young puppies (as a congenital and hereditary problem) or show up much later in life as a common orthopedic "old age" disease. Dysplasia technically means dislocation, so pets with hip dysplasia have some degree of dislocation between the ball and socket that form the hip joint. As these affected pets attempt to get up and down, and walk or run, the ball and socket components of the hip joint slip and slide around, preventing a normal weight-bearing gait. Treatment can be surgical correction or replacement of the abnormal joint, or conventional medications. In the most serious cases in older pets, euthanasia is recommended to relieve the terrible suffering and immobility that many pets with dysplasia and secondary advanced arthritis experience.

Typical of these cases, the majority of patients I have seen never had proper diagnostic testing. No radiographs of the hip joints were done in many of these dogs, or if they were taken, often the film quality was so poor as to make a proper diagnosis impossible. To take perfect radiographs of the hips, the dog must be sedated or anesthetized. This is rarely done, which makes most of the films useless when trying to diagnose any orthopedic problems in this area of the body.

Many of these poor dogs have been placed on potent nonsteroidal (NSAID) medications for many months or even years. These are powerful anti-inflammatory drugs that work very well in relieving the pain and inflammation that accompanies hip dysplasia and the associated arthritis that is often present. NSAIDs work so well that the pet should be feeling better and walking better after one to two doses of the drugs. Pets with suspected hip dysplasia or arthritis that do not show dramatic improvement after a few doses likely have another disease.

Using an integrative approach to hip dysplasia and arthritis therapy rarely requires more than an occasional dose of these powerful medications. In my practice most patients with musculoskeletal problems only receive an NSAID medication when they are having a particularly bad day. Even then, thanks to the success of integrative therapies like joint supplements, magnetic beds, acupuncture, and chiropractic, I can often dose these medications at one-half of the recommended label dose.

For those very rare patients I see that have severely advanced arthritis and can barely move, NSAID therapy might be needed on a regular basis. However, these pets receive regular (every three months) examinations and blood and urine testing to make sure the medications are not causing side effects such as GI bleeding, kidney disease, or liver disease, that are commonly seen in pets and people on long-term NSAID therapy.

To place pets on long-term therapy with potent medications like NSAIDs without a proper diagnosis, without considering other therapies, and without reevaluating the case if a response is not seen within one to two weeks of beginning the therapy is negligent and most likely malpractice. Yet my holistic colleagues and I see this type of "care" all too frequently.

Roman

Roman was a beautiful, very friendly 110-pound, male three-year-old rottweiler who limped into my practice on a beautiful spring day. It was clear from the way he attempted to move in our office that something was not right. He swayed his hips from side to side, and couldn't move for long distances before he became weak and had to plop down on the floor.

His owner, Rachel, a single twenty-something, was very

attached to Roman, who was a Christmas gift when he was just six weeks old. Rachel was slight in stature and barely weighed more than Roman. She told me that the reason for his visit was a diagnosis of hip dysplasia from his current doctor. She had read one of my pet columns in our local paper about the many uses of acupuncture, and hoped that I would be able to offer Roman help using this therapy.

In reviewing the medical records Rachel brought with her I was dismayed, but not surprised, to find that no diagnostic testing had ever been done on Roman—no radiographs or blood or urine testing, simply a physical examination to make the diagnosis of hip dysplasia. As I also expected, Roman was treated with the only NSAID available at the time of this visit, a drug called Rimadyl which Roman had been taking since his diagnosis was made, approximately three months prior to our visit. I asked her if she had seen any improvement in Roman since starting the Rimadyl. She told me that he had not shown any improvement and was getting discouraged at his lack of response and the fact that his veterinarian didn't seem interested in exploring any other treatment options with her.

I then asked her what her prior veterinarian did when she notified him of Roman's lack of response to what should have been the appropriate therapy if her pet actually had hip dysplasia. She reported that the veterinarian increased the dosage of Rimadyl! I asked her what this increased dosage did for Roman, and she said he got diarrhea, so she stopped giving him his medication. Not only had he shown no improvement when the dosage of Rimadyl was increased, he had not acted any worse since she stopped the medication several weeks prior to our visit.

At this point I knew that her dog had some type of problem that affected his mobility and ambulation, but since no diagnostic testing had been done it was impossible to say that hip dysplasia was the correct diagnosis. There were two clues that it was not. The first was Roman's failure to improve on the different dosages of Rimadyl. NSAIDs like Rimadyl are very effective medications, and if a pet does not improve when taking them, the diagnoses of hip dysplasia and arthritis are much less likely to be correct. Second, as I observed Roman trying to move around the examination room, something did not seem right. I often see a condition called degenerative myelopathy (DM) in pets misdiagnosed with hip dysplasia. DM is a progressive neurological disease, similar to multiple sclerosis in people. While dogs with hip dysplasia usually do well with appropriate therapy, the prognosis is worse for dogs with DM, which is progressive. Dogs with DM wobble in their rear legs, often crossing or dragging one or both rear legs. This condition is usually easy to suspect, and the treatment is totally different than that prescribed for pets with hip dysplasia.

Most dogs with hip dysplasia slide around the room to varying degrees, their rear legs crossing over each other. These dogs are often said to walk like someone who's had a bit too much to drink. Although they can resemble dogs with DM, they don't suffer the neurological symptoms seen in dogs with DM, and usually their gaits are characteristic of dogs with musculoskeletal problems.

Roman's gait was different, however. He didn't seem to be stumbling so much as he seemed weak, and his weakness seemed to cause his awkward gait. I didn't think that Roman suffered from hip dysplasia, or at least I didn't think that it was causing his unusual gait if he even had this disorder.

What I decided to do, instead of a hip radiograph, was run a full blood profile including adrenal and thyroid gland testing. I really suspected that some type of metabolic disease was the cause of Roman's problem. While Rachel was nervous about what this meant for Roman, I reassured her that we needed to get the right diagnosis in order to help him. She agreed, stating she just wanted Roman to get better and not suffer anymore.

I drew blood from Roman and submitted it for a spectrum of testing. At this point I didn't have a diagnosis, and Roman was not in pain, so I didn't send home any therapy for him. I told Rachel that I would be calling in a few days to discuss the results of his blood profile, and expected we would have an answer to his strange way of walking.

Two days later I got the results back and had my answer. I informed Rachel that her dear companion was not suffering from hip dysplasia, arthritis, or any musculoskeletal disease. His blood testing showed that the cause of his funny walk, his weakness, and general change in disposition was simply due to hypothyroidism. Pets with hypothyroidism suffer from too little thyroid hormone produced by the thyroid gland. The typical pet with hypothyroidism is lethargic, overweight, and sluggish, and prefers a warm environment. At least that's what we were all taught in school. Now we know that hypothyroidism can resemble a number of other problems. In Roman's case his age, breed, and size fooled his prior veterinarian into the misdiagnosis of hip dysplasia and arthritis. While it was a good guess, it was a bad diagnosis, one that literally could have been fatal to Roman if Rachel had not sought a second opinion.

Fortunately, hypothyroidism is very easily treated. For just pennies a day Roman was treated with thyroid-replacement medication. In less than twenty-four hours he was fine, as his thyroid hormone levels quickly became normal in his bloodstream.

Roman regained his strength and his walk was totally normal. Gone were his "drunken" gait and his slipping and sliding across the floor. Even though I had successfully and easily diagnosed Roman's problem, my job had just started. I worked with Rachel to get Roman on a good diet, substituting a natural food for the so-called premium diet he was eating that contained numerous by-products and chemicals. I suggested to Rachel that she stop vaccinating Roman each year, and instead do blood-titer testing to determine if and when any vaccines might be needed. Even though Roman never had fleas or ticks, Rachel was administering potent topical flea medication to him each month, and had been doing this per her prior veterinarian's recommendation since Roman was a puppy. I had her stop this as it was not necessary and was only adding to Roman's toxic load. It was also important, because Roman's breed is prone to hip dysplasia, that I take radiographs of his hips. Fortunately, these showed no signs of dysplasia or arthritis. To prevent joint problems, I prescribed a good-quality joint supplement for Rachel to administer to Roman, along with some other general health-maintenance supplements. To date Roman remains healthy, is walking normally, and is arthritis free, thanks to his daily joint supplement.

As you can tell from the representative stories in this chapter, sometimes a fatal prognosis can be overturned once the correct diagnosis, prognosis, and therapy are given. This is why second opinions are so critical when, like the pet owners whose stories you've just read, you are given a hopeless diagnosis or prognosis by your pet's veterinarian. Many times the case isn't as hopeless as it first seems, and that second opinion can offer hope for your pet.

9

Trying Something, Anything, Is Better Than Doing Nothing:

The Most Difficult Challenges

It's hard enough to help patients with severe illnesses that can't be helped by conventional means. Yet the most difficult and challenging cases are those in which a diagnosis has not been obtained.

In some cases the owner cannot afford all of the necessary testing that allows a diagnosis to be made. These cases are particularly troubling for me, as I don't believe costs should ever stand in the way of helping a pet in need. We do all we can in my practice to keep costs reasonable. Still, health-care costs continue to increase each year, for pets as well as people. While many people can afford the costs associated with the care of a pet suffering from a serious illness, some people cannot. For these folks, I highly recommend pet health insurance, which can make advanced diagnostic testing and treatments affordable for just about every pet owner.

In other situations a diagnosis has not been made despite extensive laboratory testing. These cases are particularly challenging as it's difficult to treat something when you don't know what "it" is you are trying to treat. Fortunately, these cases are very rare, as they are among the most difficult I face. Owners of these special pets are frustrated when they come for their initial visit. It's hard to convince people that modern medicine has failed to determine the cause of a pet's chronic, debilitating illness, especially when multiple doctors and specialists have reviewed the case and extensive testing has been done. These are among our most hopeless cases, as we're literally shooting in the dark as far as healing goes. While I can tell the owner all sorts of diseases the pet does *not* have, I can't tell them what the pet *has* that is causing it to be ill. These cases take all of my knowledge as well as my application of the art of medicine. No two are exactly alike, even though the treatment regimens using integrative therapies are similar for many of these very ill pets. The approach to these patients is truly integrative, as often only a combination of potent conventional medications and many natural therapies is necessary in order to offer even the slightest bit of hope for healing. Here are three special stories of how an integrative approach has helped heal pets for whom a diagnosis could not be made.

Shaggy

Shaggy was a seven-year-old male buff-colored American cocker spaniel owned by Anna. He was one of the few cocker spaniels in my practice that were difficult to handle. In years past, many cockers, especially those of the buff coloration, were very aggressive dogs. Some were so aggressive they were not allowed in the show ring as the judges could not handle them, an integral part of the judging process. This was at a time when the cocker spaniel breed was very popular, which resulted in overbreeding and inbreeding of closely related dogs. When breeders choose to mate animals for looks and appearance rather than concentrating on physical and behavioral characteristics, the result can be a mess. Fortunately, as the breed fell from popularity, the breeding improved and most cockers today are great, sweet little happy-go-lucky dogs, so typical of how the breed should act. Shaggy was not one of these happy-go-lucky guys, however. While you could pet him when he was still standing on the floor (if *he* decided he wanted you to pet him), doing any sort of physical examination or diagnostic procedure was out of the question and quite risky for the person attempting to interact with him. He would become very aggressive, attacking any hands or body parts that made it anywhere near his mouth if you needed to do something he did not want done.

To prevent injury to myself, my staff, owners, and even the pets, we usually muzzle all pets for diagnostic testing. Any pet that acts aggressively during the physical examination procedure is also muzzled, once again to keep everyone from getting bitten. While most pets do not like being muzzled, when the proper muzzle is applied correctly, it does not hurt the pet. Usually the pet is so distracted by the application of the muzzle that it becomes very cooperative when a procedure is performed, as the pet's concentration is on the muzzle and not on what we are doing to it.

Unfortunately, when Shaggy doesn't want to cooperate he becomes an extremely difficult patient and resists our muzzling attempts. Even his owner is not able to muzzle Shaggy, any attempt would result in a severe bite. Anna does, however, have an extremely long, arm-length set of gloves that she dons whenever she has to help us with Shaggy. Her routine is to grab him behind the head while one of my staff members throws a towel over his head and face. I then lift Shaggy to the table where I can perform an examination of all areas of his body except his head and face. To draw blood requires four people. After placing Shaggy on his side, Anna holds his head, still covered with a towel to keep something between his teeth and our skin. One of my assistants holds his front legs down, while the other assistant holds his hind legs down onto the table, while also occluding the vein on the outside of his upper hind leg, which I also support to draw blood from Shaggy. Once he is restrained in this fashion, he actually calms down (at least as well as he can), and drawing blood from him is then done quickly.

This is our normal routine with Shaggy, and thankfully, it only has to be done twice yearly for his regular checkups. On this particular visit, however, I encountered a very different Shaggy. Instead of his normal aggressiveness, he was very withdrawn. Anna, normally energetic and animated as she prepared to battle him for his checkup, was also withdrawn. Her eyes were reddened and still wet from crying over his condition. Anna told me that Shaggy had stopped eating and was very lethargic for the past forty-eight hours. She and I both knew something was not right.

As Anna normally does during her visits to our office with Shaggy, she put on her long gloves and helped me lift him onto the examination table. No towel was needed to be put around his head this time, as he didn't resist, growl, or in any way act aggressively toward us. I knew this was not his normal behavior and was worried that something was extremely wrong.

Anna told me she was considering euthanasia for Shaggy. A look at his medical record revealed the notation from my receptionist citing the reason Anna gave her for today's visit: in no uncertain terms, Shaggy was dying. He had not been himself for the past two days, and she didn't want to keep him alive if this was the way he was going to be. In short, she had already prepared herself for news that Shaggy was fatally ill.

I told her not to give up so soon. We didn't know what was wrong with Shaggy, and therefore any discussion of euthanasia was premature. I explained that Shaggy certainly could have a serious and even fatal problem, but we didn't know that yet. I didn't want her to give up hope until we had more information. She appreciated my honesty and admitted she was simply very scared as she and Shaggy were close and she couldn't stand seeing him in a condition she thought was terminal.

I told her that I needed to draw blood on Shaggy to get me started in trying to diagnosis the cause of his sudden change in behavior. While I assembled the troops, preparing to battle

Shaggy for a few drops of his blood, it became apparent that he was not in any condition to put up a fight with us. It was no problem to position him for drawing his blood, and it was the easiest visit we ever had with him. While that was a relief for us, it was not good news for him as something was really wrong with him to turn this monster of a patient into Gentle Ben.

While examining Shaggy I did detect a very slight heart murmur. I was not able to do a complete oral examination as I still feared he might bite, but I did notice that his gums were pale when he opened his mouth to breathe. His pale gums, in combination with the slight heart murmur, made me suspect that Shaggy was anemic, and that his sudden weakness and lack of appetite were due to a lowered red blood cell count. Shaggy had no history of poisoning or external bleeding, and nothing made me suspect he was bleeding internally. Therefore I surmised that Shaggy was either not making enough red blood cells, or that they were being destroyed in his body.

I knew I wouldn't have the results of all of my blood tests from our outside lab for at least twenty-four hours, but I wanted to know his blood count sooner to determine the severity of his anemia. Since we have laboratory equipment in our office that gives us information on basic testing, including a blood count, I had my laboratory technician Stephanie quickly run a complete blood count, or CBC, which lets me know about a patient's red, white, and platelet cell counts. It clearly showed that Shaggy was anemic as I had suspected. This is not a diagnosis, as there are many causes of anemia, and some can be fatal. Still, it was a starting point, and offered a glimmer of hope for a pet whose owner considered things were so hopeless that she had even brought up euthanasia. The good news was that Shaggy was not so anemic as to require an emergency blood transfusion.

The major causes of anemia that I think about in a dog like Shaggy include diseases transmitted by ticks (Lyme disease, Rocky Mountain spotted fever, and ehrlichiosis,) and autoimmune anemia. Any of these are possible in Texas, and I see them with equal frequency. Shaggy, however, being a cocker spaniel, was particularly prone to autoimmune anemia (specifically a condition called autoimmune hemolytic anemia, or AIHA), and there was one particular abnormality I noticed after drawing his blood. I placed a drop on a clear microscope slide. As soon as I did this, I noticed the red blood cells immediately clumped in a peculiar manner called autoagglutination, which occurs when red blood cells, coated with antibody proteins, stick to each other. That Shaggy's blood showed this autoagglutination phenomenon indicated that an immune problem was likely the cause of his acute anemia.

If Shaggy was afflicted with AIHA as I suspected, it meant that for some usually unidentifiable reason, his own immune system had gone crazy and was attacking and destroying his own red blood cells. While tick diseases, heartworm disease, and even recent vaccinations can adversely affect a pet's immune system and initiate the vicious cycle that sets off AIHA, in most cases the cause is never found.

Since we do titer testing at our office in place of traditional vaccinations, I knew that Shaggy's anemia could not be due to an adverse reaction to recent vaccination. Further testing was needed to try to determine the exact cause of Shaggy's anemia. I drew more blood and submitted it for a complete blood count and biochemical profile, requesting additional testing for tick-borne, thyroid, and heartworm diseases.

Because the blood testing would take two to three days to get all of the results, I needed to begin treatment to help save Shaggy's life pending the results and started him on two conventional drugs. The first was the antibiotic doxycycline. This antibiotic, related to tetracycline, is the recommended therapy for the treatment of the most common diseases transmitted by ticks. I knew that if Shaggy had Lyme disease, Rocky Mountain spotted fever, or ehrlichiosis, the doxycycline would start killing these infectious organisms immediately, even before his test results came back.

To stop Shaggy's immune system from attacking his own red blood cells, I needed to use aggressive immunosuppressive therapy. For AIHA, good old prednisone works well for most patients, although it has to be given in high doses in order to shut down the pet's immune system. These doses are much higher than the tiny doses I use for treating other problems like allergies in dogs and cats. At these higher doses, the chance of side effects such as infection, diabetes, pancreatitis, and GI ulcers increases. Anna was concerned about this, as Shaggy was already sick enough with his AIHA and didn't need more problems that could also prove fatal if not diagnosed and treated quickly. I assured her that I would do all I could to minimize the side effects by using an integrative approach, as supplements can help reduce the chances of side effects. However, I also told her that Shaggy needed this aggressive treatment in order to have any chance of recovery. I let her know that while some dogs with AIHA need even stronger chemotherapy to help them, and some in fact do die if their disease does not respond to any therapy, in most cases recovery occurs quickly and we should be able to reduce Shaggy's dosage of prednisone within one to two weeks if he responded as I expected.

Shaggy's treatment needed to be integrative in order to give him the best chance to survive whatever was killing him. I had to prescribe medication for the most common causes of AIHA, but also needed to use supplements to minimize the side effects from these medicines and return him to health. Because the goal of integrative therapy is to wean the pet off conventional medications as quickly as possible due to their side effects, I needed to use supplements that would have the same positive effects as the conventional medicines without their side effects.

I chose several natural therapies for Shaggy. The first was one of my favorite herbal supplements called Vibrant, manufactured by Evergreen Herbs. This is a great go-to product for pets with any illness. I have found that pets that are just not quite themselves often respond within twenty-four hours after taking this wonderful supplement. I also chose an amino-acid supplement called Liquid Amino B-plex from Rx Vitamins *for* Pets. When pets aren't eating, I believe the addition of amino acids can be quite helpful in restoring health. Cholodin, made by MVP Laboratories, is another supplement I like to use to support the liver and provide additional B vitamins, which are especially helpful for sick older pets like Shaggy.

His blood count, blood profile, and tick-borne disease test results came back two days later. Since all of his tick-borne disease testing came back negative, I had Anna stop his doxycycline as that was no longer needed. Since no other abnormalities were noted on his lab results that could explain his sudden anemia, I arrived at the final diagnosis of AIHA.

Within just one week of starting this aggressive integrative program for his immune-mediated anemia, Shaggy improved dramatically. At first, Anna needed to help him eat by hand-feeding him, and he would only eat people food rather than his own dog food. He shortly began eating dog food mixed in with the people food, however, and within a few days was back to eating his natural diet.

His laboratory results also began to show signs of improvement. His red blood cell count (called PCV, packed cell volume), which was 20 percent when he originally came in, had now increased to a respectable 30 percent. While still lower than the normal range of 35 to 55 percent, I knew it would just be a matter of time before Shaggy's PCV would return to normal. And I didn't have to wait long for that to happen. When he returned in two weeks for his next blood count, his PCV was now a more normal 47 percent. Even before I drew his blood, I knew he was feeling better. His aggressive nature had returned, and Anna was ready with her gloves to assist us in drawing Shaggy's blood. At this point, I decreased his dosage of prednisone to half of what I had originally prescribed, and continued his supplement regimen.

A recheck of Shaggy and his blood count two weeks later showed that his packed cell volume continued to remain in the normal range despite his reduced dosage of prednisone. Therefore, I continued to cut his dosage of prednisone by 50 percent every two weeks. I also stopped his Vibrant and his Amino B-plex, as they were no longer necessary, but continued with the remainder of his supplements. To provide further support for his immune system as I continued to lower his dosage of pred-nisone, I added three additional supplements that work very well to help pets with immune diseases.

The first is an antioxidant called Proanthozone by Animal Health Options, which I like to use in many of my patients with disorders of the immune system. I also prescribed a potent fatty-acid supplement for Shaggy called Ultra EFA made by Rx Vita-mins *for* Pets. This balanced fatty acid contains fish oil and borage oil and is very palatable for most dogs and cats. By reducing in-flammatory chemicals that occur as the result of cell destruc-tion, we can minimize inflammation in the pet's body and reduce damage to its immune system. Finally, I prescribed a product called Vetri-DMG made by Vetri-Science. DMG, which is short for dimethylglycine, has many wonderful healing properties and is very useful in pets with immune system disorders.

Based upon Shaggy's quick, positive response to my integrative therapy for his AIHA, and the fact that he continued to show pos-itive response as we reduced his dosage of the immunosuppres-sive drug prednisone, eventually stopping it all together, I felt good that I could heal him from this horrible and often fatal disorder. I was also happy that Anna did not have to make the difficult deci-sion to end the life of her special pet. Even though she was correct when she brought him in for his appointment and stated that he was dying, her faith in the integrative approach to his health care and her desire to do everything possible to bring him back from his near fatal disease ultimately saved him and gave her many more years with Shaggy.

To date, Shaggy has not experienced a recurrence of his anemia. He continues to feel well at home, and of course keeps us on our toes when he comes in for his biannual examinations and blood testing. Since my staff is well trained in how to handle him to prevent being bitten, I'm happy to say that so far Shaggy has never bitten any of my staff members, myself, or Anna during his visits with us. However, he did bite two employees at a local boarding facility who unfortunately interrupted him when he was eating his dinner. Thankfully, their wounds were not serious and they recovered from their confrontations with Shaggy!

While Shaggy recovered very nicely from his serious illness, enough to cause us more grief on many subsequent visits—his aggressive personality returned as soon as his anemia resolved—Anna wanted to know what she could do to prevent AIHA from returning. Despite curing Shaggy, dogs and cats that have had immune diseases are prone to recurrences. Fortunately, integrative medicine focuses on restoring health rather than simply treating disease. While we'll never know for sure why Shaggy developed AIHA when he did, it was important to make sure we did everything possible to keep him healthy and to minimize his exposure to possible toxins that might cause cell damage and cause his immune system to flare up and attack his body again.

An important part of the future care of all of my chronically ill patients is to minimize their coming into contact with anything that can cause their delicate and rebalanced systems more harm. While doctors can debate exactly what causes serious diseases in patients, there is no question that in its simplest terms, putting "bad stuff" into the pet's body has the potential to cause harm, and putting "good stuff" into it has the potential to cause health.

When the owner and I spend a lot of time trying to restore

health to a seriously ill pet, neither one of us wants to do anything to return the pet's system to a diseased one. Therefore, as I do for all of my patients, I told Anna the following: Shaggy was to have no more vaccines ever. While vaccines can certainly help protect against infectious diseases, all of the current research shows that we are vaccinating our pets way too often. Most pets rarely need vaccines after receiving their initial puppy or kitten vaccines and possibly a few boosters after that. Since anything like vaccines that adds stress to an already compromised immune system can bring my patients "out of remission/out of health," I try never to do them again unless absolutely needed. Shaggy was already eating a great natural diet, devoid of chemical preservatives and byproducts that can alter cellular metabolism, leading to inflammation and oxidation and causing cell death.

Additionally, no chemical flea and tick products were to be used unless absolutely necessary. To prevent heartworm disease, any of the monthly oral heartworm-preventive medications were fine to use. The medication in these products is given at a very low dose, and I don't have any proven natural products I can use to prevent this often fatal disease. I also don't want patients such as Shaggy, who finally go into remission and return to their road to health, to die from a preventable disease like heartworm disease.

Shaggy continues to do well and remains totally free of any drug therapy. His supplements have been reduced to a maintenance protocol, and he currently takes Cholodin, Vetri-DMG, and Proanthozone. And yes, Anna still wears her long gloves as she assists us with his regular blood drawings to make sure his AIHA stays in remission and does not return!

Bevo

While Shaggy appeared sickly when he came to me in his ane-mic state, he still resembled a normal cocker spaniel. Some pets look much, much worse. Imagine for a moment what a normal Saint Bernard looks like. This regal breed is large, big boned, very furry, with a coat that is colored with a mixture of brown, black, and white hair, and is designed to travel long distances and withstand cold temperatures.

Now imagine a sickly Saint Bernard, one whose hair is dry, lacking luster so that its coloration is dull, one who is thin, bone thin, with no obvious muscling to give it the strength that its physical appearance normally imparts. Imagine if you will, a walking skeleton. This was Bevo, the patient who was to greet me for my final appointment of the morning on that last day in Feb-ruary, as my staff and I were getting ready to say good-bye to win-ter and welcome in the spring.

I knew it was going to be a tough case. My staff members, who had already met Bevo and his owner Stan when they en-tered the office, warned me about the pitiful appearance of what should have been a beautiful, vivacious dog. My staff and I normally try to avoid euthanasia at all costs, but they were al-ready preparing me for having to offer that most humane option even before I had the chance to see the pet and review the med-ical records.

Euthanasia is a choice we fight and try not to make unless ab-solutely necessary. At least in my practice, it's the last option we ever want to offer, saving it for cases that are truly hopeless, unresponsive to any of the therapies we can offer, when attempting further treatment would constitute "cruel and unusual punishment." There are doctors who will perform "convenience euthanasia," when an owner simply does not want to treat a treatable problem, but I refuse to perform this procedure if there is any chance for the animal.

I agree that pets that are suffering and cannot be helped should not have their misery prolonged for any reason. However, many owners and veterinarians are not aware that alternative therapies might offer some hope for those cases that initially seem hopeless. In these instances, assuming the pet is neither near death's door nor suffering uncontrollably, referral to a holistic veterinarian may mean the difference between life and death for that pet. When pet owners come to me with a diagnosis of a hopeless condition, they have often been offered the option for euthanasia by a previous veterinarian and have declined, instead seeking something that can offer the pet life.

Euthanasia is difficult for all parties involved: the doctor, the staff, the pet, and of course the other family members who often must make this most difficult decision. As a result, I never take ending a pet's life lightly and only offer it when no other treatment is available to help the pet. I came up with this tough policy based upon a terrible experience I encountered many years ago, very shortly after opening my practice. To discourage convenience euthanasia, my policy was not as tough at that time as it is now, but I priced the procedure high enough to dissuade people shopping for a doctor to do the euthanasia from coming to my office. Unfortunately, one such client was not deterred by the high price of the procedure.

This particular client came in on a bright warm Saturday morning in June, less than a year after I had started my practice. He brought with him three very happy and healthy-looking terriers. My initial impression when they all walked into my office was that I would actually have some business on an otherwise slow Saturday morning. I looked forward to helping him treat whatever problems he faced with these three energetic and adorable canines.

My initial excitement quickly turned to dismay, even horror, as he requested euthanasia for all three! He said they had what he called "behavior problems," as all three dogs supposedly suffered from separation anxiety and urinated all over the house whenever he and his wife were not at home. He decided it was time for euthanasia as he could no longer tolerate these "bad behaviors."

I knew that behavioral problems were the number-one reason for euthanasia, which is why I'm such a big fan of preventing these problems as well as of very early interventions for any pets with behavioral issues. Not wanting to end the life of one, much less three, happy and healthy looking dogs, I asked about doing behavioral therapy for them. With proper training, and sometimes the use of either natural therapies or conventional medications, most dogs with separation anxiety can recover and continue to lead normal lives.

The client stated he had already tried treatment without success, and didn't want to try any more therapy.

"Well, how about letting me take the pets and find a rescue group who could work with them, fix their problems, and find new homes for them?" "Nope, not interested," responded the client. He didn't think the pets would do well separated from one another, or that anyone would adopt them, as he couldn't see how anyone could fix the pets' problems.

It was a slow Saturday, I had recently opened my practice, and needed all the business I could get. He seemed to be an honest man, and I knew behavioral problems unfortunately resulted in the death of many pets. Better that I end their lives quickly and humanely rather than let the situation continue, with the owners getting upset at the pets' problems, which the pets could not help doing, I rationalized. So that beautiful Saturday morning, in an attempt to help what seemed like a concerned owner and make some money on a day when my appointment schedule was wide open, I ended the lives of these three beautiful creatures.

That was the worst weekend in my professional life. I slept very little, wondering why I took part in those deaths. Despite my attempts to soothe my conscience by trying to convince myself that euthanasia was best for the pets, I struggled with my actions the entire weekend and for quite some time afterward.

Did I really do it to help the pets? Did I do it for the money? Was I duped by an owner I had never met who wanted a quick and permanent solution to behavioral problems I couldn't prove existed? And why did this client come to me, rather than return to his regular veterinarian who supposedly had been trying to help the pets?

After that weekend, I resolved that I would *never* again end the life of a pet unless I felt it was absolutely necessary. I would never again trust a new client who fed me some story about a pet unless I could verify it, and even then I would only agree to perform euthanasia if I felt all had been done for a case that I would label hopeless.

When my staff, which had been enforcing my euthanasia policy since I created it many years prior to seeing Bevo, actually hinted that this case might certainly fit my stringent requirements for euthanasia, I knew it was going to be especially challenging.

As I entered the examination room, fully prepared for the possibility of euthanasia rather than an attempt at therapy, I encountered a pitiful sight indeed. Instead of a typical large Saint Bernard, I encountered a creature that can best be described as a living skeleton. Based upon his bone structure, I surmised he should normally weigh about a hundred pounds. (He actually had weighed this amount until he began getting sick a few months prior to this visit, according to his owner, Stan.) Instead, my technician had recorded his weight as a mere sixty-two pounds! He was so thin that not only did his ribs and spine protrude from what little flesh covered them, but also the bones of his skull and face, normally not visible in healthy pets, stuck out. He was a walking anatomy book!

I also noticed a large amount of green discharge coming from both eyes, and long, thick, stringy saliva hung from his pendulous lips. In checking his mouth, I noticed his gums were slightly paler than the normal soft pink color typical of a healthy pet.

Despite his startling, head-turning appearance, and a generalized weakness Stan had mentioned, Bevo did manage to arise from his prone position on the cool linoleum floor of the examination room when I entered and gave me a friendly greeting, before plopping back down on the floor to continue resting his weak, tired, emaciated frame.

In examining Bevo's medical records that Stan had brought

with him, I noticed that Bevo was first seen for this exact same problem about six months before this visit. Extensive blood testing at the time by his regular veterinarian showed no problems that could explain Bevo's medical condition. His original veterinarian could find nothing obviously wrong with him, and therefore wisely referred Stan and Bevo to a local specialist. The specialist performed a few additional tests, but also could find no obvious cause for his severe clinical signs. Suspecting either an immune disease or an infectious cause for Bevo's disorder, the specialist prescribed steroids and antibiotics. He told Stan to return for more testing if Bevo did not improve, which he did not, despite the prescribed therapy, and Stan, feeling that no one could help his poor sick dog, did not return to either veterinarian for additional testing or treatment.

I knew things did not look good for Bevo. His original veterinarian and the specialist could find no cause for his condition. The treatments they had administered failed to resolve his clinical signs. Add to that the fact that Bevo had not been treated with anything for several months as Stan continued to watch his dog go downhill and I knew this would be a tough case indeed. Still, there was no way I would want to euthanize such a great dog who I'm sure used to be a magnificent creature when he was feeling better. Additionally, in discussing the difficult road ahead of us, Stan said that I was Bevo's last hope; neither he nor Bevo was ready to give up yet. If there was any chance of helping Bevo, no matter how slim or how bleak things appeared, Stan wanted to pursue it.

I knew that I could do some diagnostic testing to get started in trying to figure out what was afflicting Bevo. However, based upon the chronicity of his disease and the severity of his clinical signs, ultimately I would have to send him to a local internal-medicine specialist to get some testing done that I was not able to do at my practice. To expedite things, I decided not to do any testing that day but instead to refer Bevo to the same specialist he had seen a few months ago, when Bevo first became ill. I felt that this course of action would be in his best interest, and Stan agreed. Fortunately, with a quick phone call to the specialist's office, I was able to schedule Stan and Bevo an appointment for later that afternoon.

While I decided not to do any diagnostic testing or prescribe any conventional medications for Bevo, I did, however, want to start him on some supplements to help his overall demeanor and general lack of health. In cases like this, when a diagnosis is neither known nor readily apparent, conventional medical doctors usually place pets on what I call the "double whammy"—steroids and antibiotics. Since I thought that the specialist might do the same thing, as he had done before and as the double whammy is sometimes the best course of action pending the results of diagnostic testing, I didn't see any reason for me to do that during this visit. I also didn't want to upset Bevo's system or do anything that might negatively influence the results of any testing the specialist would perform. There was no question that Bevo did not look good. However, since he was not per se a critical case, moments away from death, I wanted to rely on natural therapies I knew could help him regardless of his eventual diagnosis.

Prior to sending Bevo on his way to the specialist for more testing, I prescribed the following regimen. First, I chose Nu-triGest by Rx Vitamins *for* Pets, a wonderful supplement to support, nourish, and heal the gastrointestinal tract. I knew that regardless of the ultimate diagnosis, Bevo was obviously not digesting his food and absorbing the nutrients necessary to maintain his weight. I also knew that the largest part of the immune system is contained within the gastrointestinal tract. Supporting the GI tract is always a good idea, no matter what happens to be the pet's underlying problem. This is a well-known principle in holistic medicine, and conventional doctors would be wise to always consider supporting the GI tract in every sick pet.

Bevo's condition is something veterinarians nickname ADR, which is short for "ain't doin' right." While conventional doctors often treat these ADR pets with antibiotics and steroids, holistic veterinarians like me prefer not to use these drugs if at all possible pending a diagnosis, unless the pet is deathly ill. While Bevo obviously was not in the best shape, I knew that taking a gentler approach by prescribing holistic supplements would be better for his health pending his visit to the specialist. Therefore I prescribed several supplements that have helped many of my ADR patients over the years.

The first of these is called Vibrant, manufactured by Evergreen Herbs, which contains several herbs to boost the pet's immune system, provide antioxidant support, and generally make the pet feel better.

Coenzyme compositum and Ubichinon compositum, two homeopathic remedies made by Heel, are also useful for pets that just aren't feeling well. They work by nourishing the cells, helping combat fatigue and slowed metabolism, relieve blocked enzyme systems, and help the pet recover from the effects of toxin buildup. These two remedies are useful whenever pets suffer from overall weakness, regardless of the condition.

Another remedy made by Heel that I prescribed for Bevo is their Detox-Kit. There's no question that pets with a chronic illness like Bevo obviously have built up toxins in their systems that continue to depress the vital functions of their cells. For these pets, a gentle detoxification using a homeopathic remedy like the Detox-Kit is a great way to help cleanse the body, specifically the gastrointestinal system, the blood and lymphatic systems, and the urinary system. It is easily administered by shaking a few drops of each of the three remedies in the kit into the pet's water.

Finally, to help reduce further oxidative damage to Bevo's cells, I prescribed the antioxidant called Super-Ox, made by Nutri-West.

I sent Stan and Bevo to the specialist with these therapies, wishing them well and telling Stan I would talk with him the next day after I reviewed the case with the specialist.

That afternoon, I spoke with the internal-medicine specialist. He had just completed his examination on Bevo and confirmed the findings from my own examination earlier that day. He also noticed that Bevo had a slight temperature. He performed a complete blood count and a blood biochemical profile, which were essentially normal except for mild anemia, which was nonspecific for any one condition. He also took radiographs of Bevo's chest, looking for abnormalities such as fluid accumulation, tumors or abscesses, and pneumonia. Fortunately for Bevo, his chest radiographs were normal and did not reveal a cause for his illness. As a result of the findings from the physical examination, laboratory tests, radiographs, and prior history, the specialist thought that the most likely diagnosis was some sort of immune-mediated disease and prescribed an immunosuppressive dose of prednisone for Stan to give Bevo twice daily.

A few days later Stan called us back to give us an update on Bevo's condition. While not 100 percent better, Bevo was feeling better, was not quite as lethargic as when Stan first brought him in to see us, had a little bit more energy, and was acting more normally. I told Stan to continue giving Bevo the dosage of prednisone prescribed by the specialist, as well as all of his supplements, and asked him to call me in two weeks to give us another update. If Bevo was still doing well and showing signs of improvement at that time, we would begin to lower his dosage of prednisone.

During the next follow-up phone call, Stan had more good news to report. While still not fully recovered from his suspected immune disease, Bevo was continuing to improve. He had just completed a follow-up visit with the specialist, who was impressed with his recovery and began lowering the dose of prednisone. I shared my excitement with Stan, knowing that Bevo was on the long, slow road to healing. I told Stan that Bevo had cleared the first and highest hurdle, having survived with his undiagnosed serious disease for many months.

Stan knew that it would take awhile, most likely many months, for Bevo to return to normal. Just as his disease had taken many months to bring him to this point, so too would healing take time to clear his body of all the toxins and help his cells begin to function normally again. I reminded Stan not to do anything to upset the healing process, such as having Bevo vaccinated or giving Bevo any other drugs or chemicals without talking with me first. Unless absolutely necessary, I never wanted Bevo to have another vaccine again in his life. Stan agreed with me that Bevo had already had one brush with death, and he did not want Bevo to go through that again!

I told Stan to continue Bevo's supplement regimen and to keep checking back with me. I expected good things for him and wanted to follow this special case. At this time it's been almost four months since I first saw Bevo. He has regained the forty pounds of weight he initially lost and is feeling great. Stan continues to work with the specialist in lowering his dosage of prednisone. Bevo once again resembles the grand Saint Bernard he was destined to be, looking nothing like the living skeleton I saw a few months ago. Thanks to Stan's patience and diligence in pursuing treatment, I look forward to seeing both of them again in my practice for many years to come.

Tarzan

Tarzan is another memorable case, for several reasons. First, he was an especially sweet rottweiler. Many of my rottweiler patients are great dogs, but some are certainly protective of family members and aggressive toward strangers. Tarzan, however, was like those rottweilers I love to see, just a real lover boy. Considering he had actually suffered abuse earlier in his life at the hands of his former male owner, he had thankfully gotten over his fear and distrust of men he didn't know. He approached me and let me pet him without showing any signs of fear or aggression so typical of abused pets that have not been properly rehabilitated.

His case history was also memorable. He had been treated for Lyme disease by his prior veterinarian about six months before our first meeting. Even though his clinical signs of weight loss, slight lethargy, mild intermittent lameness, and decreased appetite were not specific for any one disease, and despite a negative blood test for Lyme disease and other tick-borne diseases, his veterinarian still suspected the possibility of Lyme disease due to Tarzan's exposure to ticks in his environment. Treatment consisted of antibiotics prescribed by his doctor plus several over-the-counter homeopathics his owner, Tracy, had purchased at a local health-food store. He did improve and felt better for several months, but then relapsed with the same clinical signs he initially experienced shortly before our first visit.

When I saw Tarzan he was very alert and friendly. Tracy told me that he had good days and bad days, but none were what she considered "very bad" days. On his bad days he was more withdrawn and lethargic, wouldn't eat unless hand-fed, and seemed uncomfortable when moving around. He was still drinking water on his own, was playful most days for at least short periods of time, would usually go for short walks once he was able to get up and move around, and rarely had loose bowel movements. Even though his prior doctor had suspected Lyme disease, since he relapsed following his initial treatment she also mentioned the possibility of Addison's disease as a cause for his unusual clinical signs.

Addison's disease is a hormonal disease that affects people and pets (President Kennedy had Addison's disease). It occurs when the body attacks its own adrenal glands (an autoimmune disease) and causes the damaged glands to reduce the output of important hormones (cortisol and aldosterone), causing clinical signs such as weakness, vomiting, lack of appetite, and in the worst cases even shock and death, due to an imbalance of the body's own natural steroids and levels of sodium and potassium.

When diagnosed and properly treated, most patients can live relatively normal lives with the disease. The problem is that Addison's disease is extremely difficult to diagnose, and failing to do so can result in the death of the patient. Clinical signs are very vague, similar to those experienced by Tarzan. They can include intermittent weakness, lameness, vomiting or diarrhea, and lack of appetite. Pets with Addison's disease are often described by their owners as "having some bad days and then some good days." This waxing and waning of clinical signs confuses owners and veterinarians as these pets often get better on their own by the time the pet is brought to the veterinarian. Due to Tarzan's intermittent clinical signs, which recurred despite being administered the proper treatment for his suspected Lyme disease, his astute veterinarian suspected Addison's disease as a possible culprit.

The problem with trying to diagnose Addison's disease is that it resembles most other diseases. While blood testing can certainly suggest this disease, often specific testing must be done. Most pets with Addison's disease have altered electrolyte imbalances in their blood tests, with an elevated potassium level and a decreased sodium level. These pets are much easier to diagnose, as the altered blood levels strongly suggest an Addison's patient. But more and more pets have normal electrolyte levels, and to properly diagnose these pets the doctor must be extremely astute and suspicious of the disorder, as routine blood testing often fails to suggest Addison's disease as a possible diagnosis.

I knew that Tarzan's case would be challenging, not just because his disease had still not been diagnosed and treated but also because his owner had limited finances at this time.

Tracy, a nice young single parent who had been abandoned by her husband a few months prior to this visit, had also recently gone through some serious health problems. This left her recovering from a serious illness, unemployed as a newly single mom, and living with a friend while she tried to recover from her health problems and find work. I felt very bad for her and desperately wanted to be Tarzan's salvation. Despite Tracy's own troubled life, her selfless attitude kept her current focus not on her own miseries but on trying to find out what was wrong with Tarzan and fix him. She and her two young children, a handsome, brown-haired, brown-eyed ten-year-old boy and his sister, a seven-year-old blond, blue-eyed beauty who reminded me of my own daughter when she was that age, were all very strongly bonded to Tarzan and couldn't stand seeing him sick. While cost was a factor due to their recent unfortunate circumstances, they wanted to do anything possible to help return Tarzan to health so they all could live happily with him.

While I enjoy working with all of my clients and their wonderful pets, some cases touch me in a different way. I almost get personally involved with these special cases even though I still must stay somewhat detached so I can look at the case objectively (something no owner with a strong attachment to the pet can do) and make the best, most sensible recommendations to help the pet heal. But Tarzan and his family were different. I *really* wanted to help them. They had been through so much personally, with Tracy's illness and the abandonment of the husband/father. This dog just *had* to get better, as I didn't think this family could deal with yet another tragedy in the loss of this special friend. I wanted to help them by doing the best I could in restoring Tarzan's health.

Cost is always a factor in the care of a pet, and trying to help a pet like Tarzan, who had vague clinical symptoms not specific for any one disease, would not be cheap. This family had a friend who came to the visit with them and who was willing to help them bear some of the cost of care. I, too, wanted to do my best to minimize the expense. While I can't give away or discount my services, I can work with clients to design the best integrative program possible and keep costs at a minimum.

I always want to help my clients to the best of my ability, but there is always a cost that goes along with everything we do. In some cases, there is only one option. For example, a pet that has been hit by a car and needs emergency surgery must have the surgery in order to survive; there is no Plan B. For most sick pets like Tarzan, I can work with the owner to give the best possible treatment but still be cognizant of the costs involved. This approach, which I call personalized pet care, is something I developed over ten years ago. It means that each patient is unique, and that there is no cookie-cutter approach to diagnosis and treatment. It is also a very holistic approach, and the reason I can never accurately tell an owner whose pet I have not seen or whose medical records I have not thoroughly evaluated what I would do to help that pet.

In Tarzan's case, doing a specific test for Addison's would be expensive and was not yet needed. His prior blood testing, done by his previous veterinarian and provided to me by Tracy, was normal except for a slightly elevated white blood cell count. I thought the best course of action would be a complete blood profile and supportive therapy, combining both some conventional medications with several natural medicines. This truly integrative approach would be the best expenditure of Tracy's money and would give us the best shot at helping Tarzan get better so he could return to his loving family as soon as possible.

At the end of my visit with Tarzan I drew his blood and sent it to our local laboratory for testing. Despite his prior problem with an abusive male owner, he was very patient and gentle with me. He extended his right front paw when I asked for it, holding perfectly still as I inserted the needle into his cephalic vein to get the blood sample I needed.

I decided to start Tarzan on a conventional medication, prescribing the corticosteroid prednisone. While many holistic-minded pet owners are antisteroid, I feel this is the wrong attitude to take. When used correctly, as part of a holistic treatment program, steroids are wonderful drugs and are often used by holistic veterinarians. If a pet has Addison's disease, which was a distinct possibility for Tarzan, steroids can literally be lifesaving, proving the old medical saying that "No pet should die without the benefit of steroids." Even if a pet does not have a disease like Addison's, which may require steroid therapy for life, when used correctly at a low dose for a short treatment period, steroids often make the pet feel better, assist in healing, and pose little risk to the patient. Therefore, I knew that steroids had to be an important part of Tarzan's integrative treatment regimen regardless of what disease was actually causing his illness.

Of course, supplements are also an important part of an

integrative healing plan, especially when we're treating an unknown problem. Many wonderful herbs and homeopathics can also be lifesaving when used to correct metabolic and homeostatic abnormalities in sick patients, and an important part of my healing plan for Tarzan included some of these prescription supplements that have helped thousands of my patients.

To go along with his prednisone, I added two important homeopathic remedies made by Heel, Coenzyme compositum and Molybdan compositum. Both are quite useful in helping pets that just aren't feeling well regardless of the cause of their disease, assisting in metabolic functions and helping to clear toxins from the body.

This was a very special case for me, and I wanted to make sure I had a lot of follow-up contact with Tracy. I wanted regular reports, knowing that the sooner I knew if my treatment was not working, the better I could intervene and do something else. So I contacted her the day following my initial visit with Tarzan to see if things had changed after twenty-four hours of therapy.

She had good news for me. While Tarzan certainly wasn't 100 percent better, after just twenty-four hours of treatment he was starting to show signs of improvement. His appetite was better, and he would eat food that was offered to him in his bowl. It was no longer necessary for Tracy or her children to encourage Tarzan to eat by hand-feeding him. He also seemed to be more comfortable when getting up and down, to be happier and perkier and not quite as lethargic as he had been just twenty-four hours ago. I told her that this was good news. While I don't want to minimize any improvement in one of my patients, I did share with Tracy that we still had a long way to go with Tarzan. We didn't yet have a firm diagnosis, although his initial response to treatment, which included steroid therapy, was suggestive of Addison's disease.

Notwithstanding his improvement, most pets will feel better after one dose of steroid therapy regardless of their illness, and the supplements she was giving him along with his daily dose of prednisone are also designed to make pets feel better as they detoxify and heal damaged tissues. Therefore, it was way too early to know how long his improvement would last. Still, any good news is encouraging, and I asked her to continue the treatment pending our laboratory results.

The next day our laboratory had completed all of Tarzan's blood and urine testing. Most of his results came back normal, so I knew his kidneys and liver were functioning normally. He did have a few abnormalities that concerned me, however. His white blood cell count (WBC) was 33,000, an increase from the value of 21,000 that had been recorded by his original veterinarian several months earlier when Tarzan first showed his vague signs of illness. Most pet owners, and many doctors, misinterpret an increased WBC as a sign of infection. Actually, an increased WBC simply means that the patient's body needs more white blood cells. This can occur with certain medications (like steroids), as a result of the excitement and nervousness that accompanies the visit to the doctor, inflammation somewhere in the body, cancer, or infection. Simply having an elevated WBC doesn't tell us exactly why the body needs more white blood cells, only that it *does* need more, and that we must do more testing. However, whenever a blood count is done by the lab, they also do a test called a differential count that tells us the number of the different kinds of white blood cells present in the body. In Tarzan's case, there was also an increase in the number of a type of his white blood cells called band cells, or bands for short. Band cells are immature white blood cells, usually present in low numbers in the circulating blood. They are released in increased numbers from the bone marrow whenever the body really needs extra white blood cells and can't wait for them to mature properly before their release from the bone marrow. This most often occurs with infection. As I explained to Tracy, the increase in his band cells suggested an infection somewhere in his body.

I also noted a slightly decreased amount of red blood cells in Tarzan's testing. The specific test, called a packed cell volume (PCV), returned a value of 28 percent, with a normal PCV being around 35 to 45 percent. In Tarzan's case, his illness, whatever it was, caused a slight lowering of his red cells. This explained why his gums were a pale pink during his examination rather than the bright pink we associate with a healthy red blood cell count.

Tarzan also had a decreased T4 test result, a screening we use for thyroid disease, but his value was only slightly decreased at 2.6, with a normal value of around 4. I suspected that Tarzan probably didn't have thyroid disease. First, his other thyroid tests included with his blood profile were normal, and these are more accurate tests than the basic T4 test. Second, just about every pet that is sick has a decreased T4 test, so without further testing it's more likely that the lowered T4 test in a sick pet is simply the result of that pet's current illness. Still, I knew I needed to retest Tarzan's thyroid values once he was feeling better and no longer taking his prednisone, as this drug can falsely lower a T4 test.

A couple of other test values bothered me. His blood testing also showed decreased levels of albumin, a type of blood protein that carries other molecules and transports them to various tissues in the body. Albumin also maintains normal oncotic pressure, which is needed to prevent fluid from leaking out of the blood vessels into the surrounding tissue. If it goes too low, edema (fluid) builds up in the pet's chest and abdomen. Fortunately, while Tarzan's albumin level was decreased, it was not so low as to allow edema formation or result in the need for a plasma transfusion. In addition to his low blood protein, another type of protein called globulin was increased. This occurs whenever the immune system is stimulated, as globulins increase in order to form more antibodies to fight off an infection. Globulins often increase in rickettsial diseases carried by ticks, and tick-borne diseases were a concern as the suspected cause of Tarzan's clinical signs.

Finally, Tarzan's urine showed increased levels of protein, indicating a potential problem with his kidneys, which normally prevent large amounts of protein from leaving the body and spilling into the urine. I thought that this large amount of urinary protein was the explanation for his decreased blood albumin levels.

As a result of his laboratory results, I decided to add another medication to Tarzan's therapeutic regimen, doxycycline, an antibiotic that is very helpful for a variety of bacterial infections as well as in treating tick-borne diseases. While he had been treated for Lyme disease before, several months prior to this visit, Tracy told me that it was possible he continued to encounter ticks in the environment where they had lived until the past few weeks. Tracy agreed with me that even though Tarzan showed positive improvement in his clinical signs even with just twenty-four hours of his initial therapy, it was better to be safe and to use the antibiotic for two weeks just in case he had been infected with a rickettsial disease, most likely transmitted by tick exposure due to his outdoor lifestyle.

Two weeks went by before Tracy's next update. Crossing my fingers as I took her off hold and began our call, the excitement in her voice quickly allayed my concerns. Just as my staff and I had hoped, Tarzan continued to show signs of improvement. He had gained some weight, his appetite had returned, and he was eating on his own without prompting from Tracy or her children. He also was not sluggish or seem to be in pain when getting up or moving around, and even enjoyed playing with the family again. His daily walks were once again an important part of the family's normal routine. Tracy told me that she was giving Tarzan his supplements, and he had just finished his doxycycline. I shared her enthusiasm over his improvement, and told her to spend the next two to three weeks slowly decreasing his dosage of prednisone. If his condition worsened, she could easily increase the dosage of prednisone at any time.

Three weeks later, at the next update, Tracy reported that Tarzan continued to improve. She said that she tried lowering his dosage of prednisone as I had instructed, but noted that he did appear a bit sluggish if he missed his prednisone dosage for more than two to three days. I told her I was very happy with the good work she had done, and was glad Tarzan was responding to our chosen therapies. I told her to use the prednisone as needed, meaning he would probably need prednisone every few days. While this is not diagnostic for a specific steroid-responsive disease, I told her I suspected it could be an immune-mediated disease (due to the protein spilling into his urine) or possibly an unusual form of Addison's disease. I instructed her to continue the supplements he was taking as well, and as soon as it was affordable I wanted to recheck him and repeat his laboratory tests, including a test for Addison's disease, but at this point we could still wait on that, especially if cost was still an issue.

Tracy did ask about the possible need to use prednisone for the rest of Tarzan's life, hoping he would not need to take this drug much longer. I assured her that even if prednisone was necessary to keep him healthy and alive, he was on a very low dose. To alleviate any concerns she harbored about side effects that can be seen with long-term administration of steroids, I assured her that the dose Tarzan was taking was way too low to cause any problems for him.

In my years of practicing integrative medicine, it's been a rare pet that needs more than an occasional, very low dose of a steroid to control its disease. While there are some pets that need prednisone every few days, the dose is way too low to cause side effects. These pets are taking a *physiological* dose of steroid, rather than a *pharmaceutical* dose. In essence, these pets actually need a bit of steroid to keep them normal, disease free, and healthy, but the dose they take is too low to be considered a normal therapeutic dose. Since these are considered subtherapeutic doses according to the pharmacology books, I never see side effects. I told Tracy not to worry about his need for prednisone at this point, as it would not harm him and would certainly help him.

As of this writing, almost one year after my first visit with this magnificent creature, Tarzan is still doing very well, taking his supplements, and is maintained on a very low dosage of prednisone, which Tracy administers to him whenever he needs it, usually one to two times per week. On a phone call with Tracy last week she was very thankful that I was able to help her special friend. When it's affordable for her, we will recheck his blood and urine values to make sure they have returned to normal. For now, she and her kids are just so happy that Tarzan's feeling well, is on minimal amounts of conventional medication, and is a vital part of their family.

These are just a few of the many memorable cases that I see where an obvious diagnosis is not immediately apparent at the initial visit. These pets are seriously ill and might even be dying when I see them, and certainly many doctors and even some pet owners would consider their cases hopeless. Even without an immediate diagnosis, these pets can often be helped and even saved with an aggressive integrative medical treatment plan. Giving up because a case seems too tough, or a pet seems too sick, or the odds seem insurmountable and even hopeless is not in the vocabulary of a holistic doctor. Tough cases require tough diagnostic testing and aggressive therapies. I actually enjoy these challenging cases because I know the odds are often stacked against the patient's ability to heal and my ability to help the patient. When healing occurs in these difficult cases, I'm further convinced of the body's unique and amazing healing ability.

Although the owners of these special pets feel compelled with gratitude to thank me for "saving" their pets, I know that I'm only facilitating the pet's ability to heal itself. I use my knowledge and skill to show owners what to do to help their pets heal, aware that they have to do a lot of work to administer the treatments that I prescribe, and ultimately the pets must have enough healing ability to respond to the therapies. If all of these pieces of the puzzle fall into place, something truly amazing happens before our eyes. This is why I continue to be a spokesman for the pet, facing any challenge that comes my way, and believing in the value of holistic therapies to allow the miracle of healing to take place.

10

Multiple Pets, One Problem

It's distressing enough to have one pet that doctors can't help, but imagine having three pets with the same problem! That was the situation facing Jan and Harry as they realized that something needed to be done to help their family of Westies, wonderful little dogs that were miserably itchy.

A Westie Trio

As is true for many West Highland white terriers, their three dogs, Nick, Samantha, and Jeanie, suffered terribly from allergic dermatitis. Formerly playful and happy pets, typical of the breed, these poor pets didn't feel like doing much of anything other than constantly scratching, itching, and biting themselves.

Terriers are the number-one group of dogs afflicted with allergies, and Westies are the number-one individual dog breed with allergies. Allergic dermatitis is so common in the Westie breed that whenever I see one that isn't itchy, smelly, greasy, or bald, I secretly wish the pet could be bred to perpetuate all of the great qualities of this breed without the terrible affliction of allergic dermatitis suffered by most of them.

I'm often asked why so many pets seem to suffer from allergies. I think it's a combination of factors. First is incorrect breeding. We know that allergic dermatitis is a genetic condition, simply because certain breeds are over-represented when we look at which pets are more likely to develop allergies. If we keep breeding allergic pets, we'll end up with more allergic pets. The proper way to breed pets is to only breed the best specimens of that particular breed. "Best" is defined not just by looks, conformation, and how many trophies a pet has won, but by the absence of both physical and behavioral abnormalities. Proper breeding is the most important step in reducing and maybe even eliminating genetic problems such as allergies and hip dysplasia, another very common genetic problem in dogs.

Second, the allergic response is an abnormal hyperresponse of the pet's immune system. We must reduce the "bad stuff" we put into our pets, which tends to cause more inflammation and oxidation, producing the same chemicals we see in the allergic response that causes the clinical signs seen in allergic pets, and increase the "good stuff" we put into our pets' bodies in order to dampen this hyperactive immune response. Bad stuff includes many pet foods and treats on the market, high in sugars, by-products, chemicals, artificial flavors and colors, and bad fats. It includes any vaccines and chemicals the pet doesn't need, and chemicals to control fleas and ticks that most pets don't need on a regular basis. Good stuff includes healthy meats, grains, vegetables, and fruits (organic when possible) that many manufacturers of natural pet food and treats use. Good stuff also includes high-quality supplements such as fish oil, enzymes, antioxidants, green foods, and health-maintenance formulas.

Finally, we live in a toxic world. While it's not possible for most of us to move to a pristine, pollution-free town, anything we can do to reduce air pollution will help all pets and people stay healthy. Reducing air pollution in our homes is also important. Regularly changing air filters, frequent vacuuming and cleaning the house, cleaning the pet's bedding, regular bathing of the pet, reducing the use of sprays (hair spray, perfumes, etc.) in the presence of the pet, and, of course, not smoking in the house (and preferably not at all) will reduce allergies and other health problems in pets, as well as in their owners. When you keep in mind that most allergic pets and people overreact to multiple allergens (house dust mites, animal fur, dander, and saliva, various grasses and trees, ragweed and other pollens from flowering plants, and molds and fungi), it's not surprising that allergies affect so many pets and people or that they can occur any time during the year (although fall and spring seem to be the most problematic for the majority of allergy sufferers).

Jan and Harry, a middle-aged, childless couple, happened to be fans of my award-winning radio show, *Dr. Shawn—The Natural Vet*, on Martha Stewart Living on Sirius Satellite Radio.

They had listened for a few months, and knew that I frequently discussed natural therapies for allergies, probably the most common condition I see here in Texas. Since it's not just a condition unique to Texas, most of my radio-show listeners can relate as they and their furry family members suffer from allergies. Jan and Harry lived a few hours away from my office in Plano. None of their local veterinarians were able to help their brood, and they decided to make an appointment with my office to see if I could offer them any hope for their once playful and happy Westies. Starting their midmorning visit that Thursday morning, I welcomed the gang to our office, thanking the couple for caring enough about their pets to make the three-hour drive. Jan and Harry immediately struck me as easy-going people. As I watched them interact with their three Westies I could see they were very fond of these special dogs.

An important part of my physical examination, especially when the problem involves a skin disorder, is to examine the pets visually from a distance, before I ever approach them and start the hands-on examination. This serves two purposes. First, while not rushing up and immediately putting the pet on the examination table, the pet has a few minutes to become comfortable with me. Let's face it: like people, most pets don't really like going to the doctor. It's scary, the doctor is poking, and sometimes uncomfortable or painful procedures (sticking a thermometer or needles into the pet) need to be done. Rushing right up to the pet is perceived as an aggressive move on the part of the doctor, and the pet feels challenged. It will either become submissive, often urinating on the floor or table, or become protective and act aggressively toward the doctor. Ignoring the pet before I interact with it prevents this reaction. Most of my furry patients actually enjoy coming to our office as I let them approach me after becoming comfortable with the "stranger in the strange room."

Second, I like to look at the whole pet (hence the term "holistic practice") before I look at its parts. By standing back and just watching I can learn a lot. For pets with skin problems I get to see all of the skin and hair on the body. During the initial few minutes of the visit I can observe if the pet is itchy, and how much it scratches or licks and bites itself. I can tell if there is any odor in the room, which can indicate a skin infection or seborrhea. So, as I began our visit, I mainly talked with Jan and Harry, inquiring about the condition of their Westies and reviewing the medical history they brought for me. During the conversation I was also keeping my eyes on the dogs, making notes about their appearances and looking for signs of itching.

Compared with many Westies I see with skin disease, these three dogs looked pretty good. Many of my allergic Westie patients look quite pitiful. They are often totally bald (or pretty close) from hair loss due to their chronic itching and skin infections. Many have dark black skin rather than the normal pink skin typical of most breeds of dogs; the darker, hyperpigmented skin is the result of months or years of chronic dermatitis. A good number of Westies with skin disease are also greasy and very smelly; these dogs typically have infections secondary to their chronic allergies, usually bacteria, yeasts, or both. Fortunately, Nick, Samantha, and Jeanie looked much better than most allergic Westies.

All three dogs had various degrees of hair loss and mild inflammation, but they were not even close to what one would describe as "bald dogs." I also noted a slight odor during my examination. Closer inspection revealed that while the skin had a mild odor and a bit of greasiness, most of the odor was actually coming from their ear canals. Typical of many allergic dogs, these three Westies had fought chronic ear infections for several years. Jan and Harry expressed their frustrations over constantly fighting these infections. They hated to see their pets suffer from chronic itching and ear infections, and they knew that, while cooperative, their pets really didn't want to have pills forced down their throats multiple times each day for the remainder of their lives. They were right to be concerned about the quality of life these pets experienced, as the pets hadn't seemed happy in a very long time.

I pursued the problem of the chronic ear infections as I knew this was a big concern for Jan and Harry. As they shared with me, while various ear drops and ointments that had been prescribed by prior veterinarians temporarily resolved the infections, invariably they would return shortly after stopping treatment. As I explained, there were several reasons the ear infections never really went away.

First, it's really important that the doctor do a proper ear cleaning before treating the infected ears. If this is not done, the pet leaves the office with dirty, smelly, and often painful ears. As a result, the pet won't let the owner properly treat these painful ears at home, and most owners don't relish the thought of dealing with them. Getting the ears cleaned at the office means the owner has a much easier job of continuing the prescribed therapy at home. While most pets can be awake during the procedure, for some, sedation or anesthesia is a must as it's just too painful to clean the ears while the pet is awake.

Moreover, there's no way any medication, natural or conventional, can make its way down the two ear canals (vertical and horizontal) present in dogs and cats when the pathway is blocked by a bunch of infected debris. If the ears are not cleaned prior to treatment, it's almost impossible to ever heal the pet by curing the infection.

Second, it's also important, prior to flushing the ears, to examine a swab of the ear debris under the microscope. While doctors may be able to correctly guess the cause of the ear infection most of the time, it's impossible to be accurate 100 percent of the time through guessing. This swabbing should be standard practice prior to obtaining a definitive diagnosis of the cause of the ear infection, but for reasons I still don't understand many doctors don't do this, preferring to rely on an educated guess. My clients don't want to pay me to guess at the cause of their pets' problems; instead, they want a definite answer. So by examining a stained smear of the ear debris microscopically, I can then inform them of the exact cause of the infection and pick the treatment that is most likely to resolve the infection.

As I discussed the ear infections with Jan and Harry, they both confirmed that no ear flushing had ever been done on any of the pets, and certainly none of their previous doctors had done a microscopic examination of the ear debris. Therefore, my technician Lynn took an ear swab from each dog, stained it with a microbiological stain, and confirmed my suspicions of a yeast infection called malasseziasis in all three dogs.

Following the diagnosis of a yeast ear infection, it was time to prepare the Westies for their medicated ear flushing. Once again Lynn took each dog to the treatment room, assisted by a college preveterinary student named Alicia who was working at our practice at the time. The ear flushing consists of three steps. First, a liquid solution is placed in the ears to loosen up the infected debris, making it easier and less painful for the second step, in which a medicated solution is gently flushed and then removed from each ear using a bulb syringe (the same type parents often use to remove mucus from a child's nose). The third step utilizes an herbal ear solution that is placed into each ear and left there to help kill the yeasts.

Nick, Samantha, and Jeanie were great little dogs, very patient and cooperative during the ear-flushing procedure. Thankfully, their ear infections were not too severe at this visit, and since these dogs did not experience any pain or discomfort during the ear flushing procedure, all three were able to remain awake.

While the Westies were in the treatment room having their infected ears carefully cleaned, I reviewed the history of their allergies and ear infections, and the entire clinical picture became quite clear. I explained to Jan and Harry that their dogs were genetically predisposed to allergies. Allergic skin is not normal and is more likely to become infected, explaining their chronic ear infections. By focusing on healing the allergies, the ear infections should resolve as well. Even though Nick, Samantha, and Jeanie would experience flare-ups of itching and infections in the future, these should occur infrequently, and minimal medication would be needed to keep the pets healthy and control their infections. Jan and Harry were very excited to hear that although a cure was not possible for their pets' genetic allergy problems, Nick, Samantha, and Jeanie would not suffer miserably from itching and ear infections for the rest of their lives.

The microscopic stains of the ear debris from the dogs each showed an infection with the yeast malassezia, a common pathogen I see in many allergic dogs (especially Westies) with ear or skin infections. While conventional doctors typically treat yeast ear and skin infections with potent antifungal drugs such as keto-conazole or itraconazole, I have never had to use these very potent and expensive medications. The holistic approach works very well in treating many forms of yeast infections in dogs and cats, and is much safer and less expensive than using these potent drugs.

Finally, I noticed that Nick had some pustules (pimples) and papules (scabs that form on the top of tiny red bumps) along his spine. This allowed me to diagnose a bacterial infection of the skin commonly seen in miniature schnauzers, called schnauzer comedone syndrome, similar to acne seen in people. While Nick was not a schnauzer, he still had the same problem that affects so many dogs of the schnauzer breed. In addition to his other skin problems, I also would have to treat this medical issue.

After having developed a diagnosis of allergic dermatitis with secondary seborrhea caused by a yeast (malassezia) infection, I was able to formulate a treatment protocol that I felt would be very helpful in returning these pets to normal.

While I don't like to use conventional medications more than absolutely necessary, I find that in many of my allergic patients I must use small amounts of an anti-itching drug like prednisone. I use very low doses (much less than the medical textbooks say are needed) just long enough to keep them "comfortably itchy" while the owner and I wait for the natural therapies to kick in and start healing the pet. I advised Jan and Harry to give a low dose of prednisone for just a few days to make their pets comfortable.

Antioxidants are very important in reducing the inflammation seen in allergic pets. I prescribed a product called Proanthozone from Animal Health Options that has helped a lot of my allergic patients.

Fatty acids are also noted for their ability to heal inflamed, itchy skin. While I have several favorite products I typically prescribe for my allergic patients, Jan and Harry were already giving their pets a good-quality fish-oil supplement that had been prescribed for them by their regular veterinarian. As is typical of conventional doctors, the dosage prescribed for the pets was far too low to help with itching but instead is a dose used to maintain a healthy coat. I prescribed a dosage I felt would better help change the chemistry of the cell membranes to make them less likely to produce the chemicals that cause itching in allergic pets.

Herbs are also very helpful in allergic pets. Some veterinarians prescribe individual herbs, but I prefer balanced formulas that contain multiple herbs to help reduce inflammation, decrease itching and redness, and support the pet's immune system. One that has worked well for many of my patients is a product by Nutri-West called Sino Formula. This potent herbal product, which I use to help many of my very itchy allergic patients, contains a number of Chinese herbs such as Chrysanthemum Ye Ju Hua, Forsythia Lian Qiao, Lonicera Jin Yin Hua, Angelica Bai Zhi, Magnolia Xin Yi Hua, and Glycerrhiza Gan Cao, designed to support the immune system and liver and to reduce symptoms often seen in allergic patients.

Conventional medicine must resort to pretty potent drugs to kill yeasts and bacteria, and I occasionally must also use these medications for severe, potentially life-threatening infections, but most skin infections can be easily treated with natural antibiotics and antifungal preparations. I've had great success in treating skin and ear infections caused by yeasts with the product from Vetri-Science called Oli-Vet, an olive leaf extract that has potent antifungal properties and assists in supporting proper immune function. Oli-Vet is one of my favorite supplements to treat mild bacterial, fungal, or yeast infections in pets when I don't want to use conventional medications. Even when I need to use potent antibiotic medicines, using additional natural antibiotics like Oli-Vet allows me to use less conventional medication and to prevent frequent relapses of the infection.

After thoroughly flushing the ears of all three dogs, I prescribed a natural herbal product that I've used successfully for pets with yeast and bacterial ear infections, the herbal ear wash product simply called Ear Care from Espree, which contains three herbal oil extracts (tea tree, eucalyptus, and peppermint oils), smells great, and is very easy to administer to most pets. Because of the slight greasiness and smell of the dogs' skin (caused by the presence of the yeasts), as well as Nick's mild case of acne on his back, I prescribed a canine benzoyl peroxide shampoo. Jan and Harry were instructed to bathe each pet daily for one to two weeks with this shampoo, which would remove the greasiness from the skin and flush the acne lesions. I made sure to tell them to leave the shampoo on the dogs for about ten minutes before rinsing, as increased contact time is needed to kill the infection. While I knew it was asking a lot for this busy couple to bathe all three dogs each day, they assured me they would find the time to do so if it would help the pets heal.

For maintenance bathing of Nick, Samantha, and Jeanie, I prescribed an aloe vera/colloidal oatmeal shampoo and conditioner. Jan and Harry were to use this as needed for itching, but I told them to expect that they would need to bathe each pet one to three times per week to control itching and keep them "comfortably itchy" and free of infections.

The final supplement that I prescribed was a product called Vim & Vigor by Pet-Togethers. A flavored chewable treat for dogs and a flavored powder for cats, it is one of my most frequently prescribed supplements for just about any problem. Originally I began using Vim & Vigor for all of my normal patients to help them maintain a healthy immune system. The numerous ingredients in it also provide support for the gastrointestinal system, bladder, and joints. I found it very useful in keeping my healthy patients healthy, seeing fewer problems in pets taking the twice-daily supplement. I also began prescribing it for new puppies and kittens, as I discovered it helped reduce anxiety in these pets and let them sleep more comfortably at night.

As my experience with Vim & Vigor increased, I started using it as part of my holistic therapies for pets with illnesses as well. Since I saw really good responses in many of my allergic patients, I prescribed it for Nick, Samantha, and Jeanie to complete my treatment protocol.

And for the comedones (pimples) I saw on Nick's back, I didn't add any extra supplements. Since his condition was pretty mild, I was confident that the supplement and bathing regimen I prescribed for all of the pets would also work for him.

With an explanation of my allergy, ear, and antiyeast protocol, and all necessary supplements in hand, I wished Jan and Harry well and told them to have a safe drive back home, asking them to please update us on how their wonderful Westies were doing after a few weeks on the holistic treatment plan. They both thanked me for my time, excited about the possibility of finally healing these pets once and for all without using any more conventional medications.

I see so many wonderful people and pets in our office, and it's easy to forget just who I've seen recently. However, I didn't forget this special case. It's not often I see a family with three pets of the same breed, all affected with the same condition. I really hoped that this natural approach would help all three. I knew that, based upon treating thousands of pets with allergies, the holistic approach definitely works. It may take six to twelve months of therapy (the same amount of time necessary to determine if conventional "allergy shots" work, by the way) to accurately determine what's working, and the treatment plan may need to be modified, but I knew that with the exception of two pets in many years of practice who showed only minimal improvement using natural therapies plus multiple conventional medications, with patience and persistence all of my allergic dogs and cats improved using a natural approach.

Fortunately, Jan and Harry had very good news when they called me one month following their initial visit. All three dogs were taking their supplements as prescribed, and they seemed to like their regular bathing regimen. Only a few doses of prednisone needed to be given to help them with their itching. Hair was regrowing and body and ear odors were gone. The best news was that they were now also feeling better! They were more playful, asked to go on their walks, and seemed more interested in life. The three were now acting like how healthy Westies should act.

It's been two years since I first saw this wonderful family, and to date, all three dogs continue to do well. While they have seasonal flare-ups common to most allergic pets, for the most part they don't itch any more than normal pets. Since allergic dermatitis is a genetic disease, we know that we can't cure Nick, Samantha, and Jeanie. What we can do, and have done, is control their allergies with minimal use of conventional drugs. Thanks to changing their internal biochemistry through the use of natural supplements and a natural diet, they only have problems when the environmental allergens are really bad, usually just for a short time in the fall and spring.

Jan and Harry continue to keep their brood healthy with the regimen of a great diet, bathing as needed, and administration of the supplements I prescribed. By not vaccinating their pets unless titer testing indicates a need for additional immunizations, and by not using conventional medications unless absolutely necessary, these pets continue to be itch free most of the year and to stay in excellent health.

11

Old Age Is *Not* a Disease

All veterinarians develop a special interest in an aspect of pet care. For some (but definitely not me), it is surgery. Other doctors really like dentistry, or get excited about animal behavior. I like integrative medicine (obviously), exotic pet medicine, dermatology, and internal medicine. I also have a special love for geriatric medicine, a growing field of specialization in veterinary medicine.

Over the last ten years, both the human and veterinary fields of medicine have seen more and more doctors interested in caring for the older segment of the population. As is true with younger patients and the field of pediatrics, older patients also require special care, and just as pediatrics is not particularly appealing to many doctors, neither is geriatrics, and many doctors are not particularly thrilled about working with older people—or pets.

What constitutes an older pet? While there are various opinions on the correct age that we should label a pet as "older," "middle-aged," or "geriatric," I like to keep things simple. In my practice, we start doing examinations and laboratory evaluations twice yearly rather than annually at five years of age. Certainly this is not a true geriatric age for most pets except for giant breeds of dogs like Great Danes, but five is approaching middle age for many cats and dogs. Most of my patients ten years and older have a significant number of degenerative conditions that must be addressed before they progress to the point where any treatment may bring diminishing results. Since I like to catch diseases before they become clinically apparent and possibly harm the pet, I chose five years of age as our magic number to start being more aggressive in trying to prevent diseases commonly seen as pets age.

Unlike many doctors, I really love working with older pets. I'm not really sure how I developed this interest in geriatric medicine. Maybe it's because I see so many older pets that other doctors either can't help or just don't want to help. It's hard to believe that doctors don't want to spend time with this group of patients, and certainly a lot of time is often required with each patient as many geriatrics have multiple problems that need to be addressed.

Nevertheless, a large majority of these older pets do remarkably well when treated properly. Many doctors give up on them, discouraging pet owners from pursuing aggressive therapies due to the pet's advanced age or the cost of pursuing diagnosis and treatment. There's a term human emergency-room doctors use when dealing with many frequent visits by the senior citizen sect. It's called GOMER, and it means "Get Out of My Emergency Room," a not-so-nice term these doctors use to express their frustration with older patients who are always in the emergency room for one thing or another. Rather than being frustrated with this special segment of the population, why not refer them to someone who really wants to help these patients, offering geriatric patients the same special care they were offered during their more youthful times?

My general approach to pet care is the same regardless of the pet's age. I do not make financial decisions for my patients and their families. It's the owner's decision on what to do and what to spend on each pet's care. My job is always to prescribe the best care for the pet regardless of age, procedure needed, and the cost of the care. I work with owners to make the best decision, discussing all of the things that need to be done and making sure the owner understands all aspects of the pet's required care.

Sometimes I am very blunt during these discussions. While I never want an owner to opt not to do treatment for a pet due to age, it's still important that age and expected longevity be taken into consideration.

As an example, an owner of an older pet with arthritis has many choices to help the pet. A total hip replacement for a damaged hip joint might be the best therapy, but it is not always practical for a thirteen-year-old golden retriever living on borrowed time. Many owners of these older pets are aware that the pets could easily pass away in their sleep simply due to old age, and it's hard to make a case for spending a large amount of money to cure a disease that might never result in a pet's death.

If a pet were half the age of these seniors, many owners would spend the money to provide this solution as it is the only one that actually cures the problem. Instead, while the owner of the older pet needs to at least consider a total hip replacement, most will choose therapies such as joint supplements or acupuncture. These therapies are designed to keep the pet comfortable and relatively pain free, helping it to live out its remaining life with good quality. In short, these pets will die *with* their diseases, but not *from* their diseases. This approach is very holistic in caring for our aged patients, still treating them humanely but not going overboard.

Still, every owner is different, and I support my clients in whatever decisions they make. The stories I've selected for this chapter are about these special pets whose owners were faced with the difficult decision of just how much care their pets needed. Each owner made what he or she felt was the right decision at the time based upon the age of the pet, the cost of care, the diagnosis, and the prognosis I gave. While each case is different, they all show that using an integrative approach to health care was the best for each pet.

Sadie

Sadie's case was typical of many geriatric patients. She had multiple problems and had been on several medications to control them. Although not as bad as the situation with many older human patients, Sadie was still a victim of conventional medicine. She suffered from what we call "poly-pharmacy." This term implies that multiple medications are needed to control the various problems a patient has. It all starts so innocently. An older patient has a medical problem, goes to the doctor, and is given one or several medications. Unfortunately, sometimes the medications cause more problems for the patient, and more medications are given to control these new problems. Then another disease pops up and even more medications are administered. When side effects from these medications arise—you guessed it— even more medications are given to control the side effects! This is a never-ending, vicious cycle. If an integrative doctor doesn't intervene and attempt to replace some of these medications with more natural therapies, the pet becomes a pharmaceutical cripple, eventually succumbing to treatments that are worse than the original disease. While Sadie had not yet progressed to this point, without some help she was on her way.

Sadie was a beautiful spayed female twelve-year-old Swiss mountain dog with multiple problems. She suffered from seizures (thought to be due to epilepsy), arthritis (manifested by occasionally walking stiffly), urinary incontinence, inflammatory bowel disease (IBD), and a tumor near her heart (present for some time but not then causing her any problems).

To control these various problems, Sadie's owner, Brenda, had consulted with several veterinarians, including various specialists. Sadie's current daily conventional medical therapy included several medications prescribed by these veterinarians and, thankfully, a few supplements that Brenda found via her own research.

Sadie was currently taking phenobarbital, a common anticonvulsant medication, twice daily to help control her seizures. She had been on this medication for several years since her initial diagnosis. She was also taking two drugs to control her IBD, metoclopramide and famotidine. One of the veterinarians with whom Brenda consulted prescribed another drug called phenylpropanolamine (PPA) for her urinary incontinence.

Thankfully, the various doctors treating Sadie recognized that phenobarbital can cause liver disease as a side effect. Because of this Sadie regularly had her blood checked. The only abnormality her veterinarian detected in her blood was an increased level of an enzyme called alkaline phosphatase (SAP). Her veterinarians felt that this indicated liver disease, but they did not alter her dosage or stop the administration of the phenobarbital.

While many conventional doctors would have placed a dog like Sadie on NSAID medications to relieve the pain and inflammation caused by her arthritis, due to her so-called liver disease the doctors did not want to place Sadie on any of these medications, as they can cause liver problems as a side effect.

Brenda was also doing a few natural things to help Sadie, giving her a weekly massage to help with her arthritis. She had also requested weekly injections of a natural therapy called Adequan Canine from her veterinarian. Adequan injections can be very helpful for pets like Sadie who have arthritis, and usually cause no side effects. Brenda was hoping that I would be able to prescribe additional supplements to help Sadie's arthritis, or maybe even recommend acupuncture for her to provide additional relief of pain and inflammation and to encourage healing of her arthritic joints.

One of the doctors who had treated Sadie for her various problems recommended several nutritional supplements that she thought could help Sadie. These included MSM (a sulphur-containing product often prescribed for pets with arthritis); Cosequin (a natural joint supplement made by Nutramax Labs); omega-3 fatty acids (useful to maintain general health and for any type of inflammatory condition such as arthritis); L-carnitine (a supplement often used to help pets with heart disease), and CoQ10 (an antioxidant that is also useful for pets with heart disease).

This was quite an involved case, and I knew I would have my work cut out for me. Not only did I have multiple diseases to address, but also I needed to do things to help Sadie regain health, while at the same time trying to reduce her need for all of her medications. Since so many things were interrelated, it was hard to know where to begin. As I often do, I had to jump back and forth between problems and medications in discussing these things with Brenda, so she could make sense of everything.

I began with the first problem Brenda had brought up, Sadie's history of seizures. She had been diagnosed with epilepsy, which is a term we give to patients with seizures whose exact cause cannot be identified. Sadie had already been through a lot of diagnostic testing to make sure she did not have any other known causes of the seizures, such as an infection or a brain cyst or tumor. Fortunately, Sadie had been seizure free for quite some time, probably due to her phenobarbital medication. Because of this, I suggested that it would be possible to slowly decrease and, hopefully, eventually stop the phenobarbital medication, replacing it with supplements that have helped many of my seizure patients in the past.

I then turned my attention to her alleged liver disease. Her previous doctors had suspected liver disease based upon the

SAP enzyme that had been elevated on all of her blood tests. (Surprisingly, though, they did not attempt to replace her phenobarbital medication, which can cause liver disease, with another, safer anticonvulsant medication.) I, however, suspected that the elevated SAP was not due to actual liver damage but was in fact a result of enzyme induction due to her chronic use of phenobarbital, which, like prednisone, can cause liver disease but can also elevate certain enzymes including the SAP via a biochemical reaction called enzyme induction. Since Sadie's other blood values, including those commonly used to diagnose liver disease (the ALT and GGT), had always been normal on her blood tests, I did not really believe she had any problems with her liver. Still, it would be important to try to reduce and eventually eliminate her need for phenobarbital to prevent problems that could arise with her liver at any time. While she continued taking phenobarbital until the time came when we could eliminate her need for it, she would need supplementation to help support and protect her liver.

Brenda had brought Sadie to me to discuss the possibility of doing acupuncture for her arthritis. While Sadie was taking several supplements that seemed to help, Brenda wondered aloud if there was anything more we could do to help her. I told her that acupuncture would be a possibility, but I personally prefer to prescribe supplements for my arthritic patients. While acupuncture can be very helpful, it involves multiple visits to our office that can be difficult for the pet and the pet owner. I told Brenda that there were a few additional supplements we could use to help Sadie that might be more effective than acupuncture and provide some more relief, above and beyond what Brenda was already giving her.

I also told her that if Sadie had painful days, we could use drugs like NSAIDs in a holistic way that would provide Sadie relief without causing side effects. While Sadie's other doctors were concerned about using these drugs because of what they called her liver disease, I was not at all concerned since Sadie obviously did not have liver disease. Additionally, other medications, in the same family as morphine, could also be used to help control pain if we needed to do that at some point.

I was quite blunt with Brenda and told her that Sadie, being an older, large-breed dog, was nearing the end of her expected life span. My goal for these special pets is to keep them comfortable, using a minimal amount of medication needed to do so. If, however, more drugs are needed to keep these older pets comfortable, we would do that in order to extend their lives and give them more time with their families. While side effects of medications are very rare when they are used in a holistic fashion, we have to accept that side effects, including severe and even fatal ones, may occur. However, my approach is to give family members as much quality time as possible with their older pets. I would much rather take the slight risk of causing death due to severe side effects from a prescription drug at some point down the road, rather than end that pet's life today from euthanasia due to the severity of the pet's disease, simply because an owner fears possible but fortunately rare side effects of medications.

Brenda also asked about the medications she was giving Sadie to control her IBD. She was currently administering two drugs, metoclopramide and famotidine. Metoclopramide is usually given to pets for two reasons. It's a wonderful antiemetic drug that quickly eliminates vomiting in most pets. Its second use is for pets with a slow GI system that need help moving food along their GI tracts.

There's really no reason for a pet with IBD to take this drug, however. Until the cause of the IBD is addressed, the most metoclopramide will do is minimize but not eliminate vomiting. Nevertheless, in most cases the drug is ineffective or only minimally effective in pets with IBD, as the inflammation that causes the problem continues despite taking this drug. Additionally, metoclopramide should really not be used in pets with a history of seizures, as it can cause further seizures. While Sadie had not suffered any side effects so far, it was really important that we try to get her off her metoclopramide as soon as possible to prevent future seizures.

Famotidine is an antiulcer medication. Although it can be helpful when used in the short term for pets with proven or suspected ulcers, as is the case with metoclopramide, there is really no reason to prescribe this for pets with IBD like Sadie. I told Brenda I would prescribe some natural supplements to help Sadie's IBD, and that we would take her off these two medications within a few weeks of administering her supplements.

Sadie was obviously a dog with multiple problems. While she had been prescribed a number of medications to help her with these problems, they really weren't necessary and might have been contributing to her overall lack of health. Sadie was typical of many of the older pets I see that are misdiagnosed, treated inappropriately, and fail to get better. Owners continue to spend money on treatments that don't work as they watch their pets' health further decline. Someone or something must intervene in this process or the pet will succumb to its diseases or treatments, or both. Fortunately, these are the types of cases for which integrative medicine works best.

I knew that we would need to decrease and eventually stop as much of Sadie's prescription conventional medications as possible. I also knew that I needed to come up with a supplement regimen for her that would replace these medications and restore her health. Brenda understood that we were not looking for a miracle, and that Sadie was an older dog who would continue to have old-dog problems. She shared with me her goals of making Sadie happy, healthy, and as normal as possible, considering her old age and multiple health issues. I told Brenda that these were good, realistic goals that I felt we could achieve for her and Sadie.

I first addressed Sadie's arthritis. Although Brenda was already giving Sadie good supplements to help her joints, she still experienced some stiffness on certain days, especially when it was cold or wet outside. I added a product from MVP Laboratories called CholoGel. Easily applied to the pet's food, it is a powerful hyaluronic acid supplement that works well for pets with arthritis, even when they don't respond as expected to other joint supplements.

I also prescribed another product from MVP Laboratories called Cholodin. This supplement is administered as a flavored chewable treat and is very useful for several conditions. First, it would provide the liver support and protection that was needed while Sadie continued to take her phenobarbital medication. Second, it is also one of my favorite supplements to use in pets with seizures. Finally, it's a great geriatric supplement that in my personal research has shown to decrease the incidence of cognitive disorder (Alzheimer's disease) in dogs and cats. It was a perfect supplement for Sadie.

To provide additional support for her liver, and to help minimize seizures as we began to lower Sadie's dosage of phenobarbital, I added a supplement from Vetri-Science called Vetri-DMG. Hepato Support, from Rx Vitamins *for* Pets, was also added to her treatment protocol to provide additional support and protection for her liver.

Even though Sadie had not experienced any flare-ups of her IBD, her other doctors had treated her with the wrong medications and had not addressed the underlying cause of her problem. Therefore, I prescribed two supplements for Sadie, NutriGest and RX Zyme, manufactured by Rx Vitamins *for* Pets, that work amazingly well for most of my patients who have IBD.

Brenda had asked about acupuncture for Sadie at the start of our visit, but we decided against it due to the distance she and Sadie would have to travel several times each week to come to our office for treatment. I also told Brenda I expected that Sadie would be walking normally again very soon as a result of the additional joint therapies I prescribed for her.

With this information, the additional supplements, and the new-found hope that Sadie would soon return to the dog she had been before all these medications had been prescribed for her, Brenda and Sadie said good-bye to me and left for their trip home.

When my technician called Brenda a few weeks after our initial visit with Sadie, Brenda reported that Sadie was doing very well. Her stiffness was mostly gone, and she walked without pain or discomfort most days. Brenda was giving Sadie the supplements as I prescribed, but had not yet decreased her levels of prescription medications. Brenda wanted to give Sadie a few months of stable health just to make sure she would not have any problems as she decreased her conventional drugs. I did not have a problem with that, but did tell her that I would like to start decreasing them as soon as possible, especially her gastrointestinal medications, which might have contributed to her seizures. I reassured her that I expected our holistic approach to Sadie's care would work very well and did not anticipate any problems as she started to decrease her medications. If Sadie did experience any flare-ups of her IBD or began seizing again, we could always start her back on her conventional medications. I asked Brenda to keep in touch as we attempted to put Sadie on a totally natural protocol that would keep her healthy and control her multiple medical problems.

During the next few months, Sadie continued to enjoy her newfound level of improved health. At this time, she is doing well on her natural treatment regimen. Brenda has stopped most of Sadie's conventional medications; Sadie is currently on a low dosage of phenobarbital, and soon will be totally off this medication if she continues to do well and does not experience a recurrence of her seizures.

Looey

While Sadie was a fairly healthy older dog who simply had a number of problems commonly seen in geriatric pets, some pets have more serious disorders.

Looey was a twelve-year-old neutered male shepherd-cross. Unlike many shepherds who seem to have multiple health problems throughout their lives, his owner, Rick, shared with me that Looey had been healthy his entire life. About a year earlier, Rick noticed a tiny spot on Looey's right nostril that seemed unusual. No bigger than the tip of a pencil, it appeared simply as a slightly pale spot of discoloration on Looey's otherwise black nostril. Because it didn't seem like a big deal or bother Looey, Rick didn't think much about it and ignored it for about a month. When it didn't go away and started to increase in size and to scab over, Rick decided it would be best if Looey's veterinarian took a look at it.

The veterinarian examined the lesion and agreed with Rick that it probably wasn't anything to worry about at that time. He thought it might be a bug bite or some sort of healing wound from where Looey might have scratched himself. The veterinarian prescribed an antibiotic-steroid ointment for Rick to apply to the lesion two to three times a day, told Rick to use the ointment for several weeks, and to let him know if the tiny lesion did not heal.

Rick took Looey home, relieved that this lesion didn't really amount to anything serious. He dutifully applied the ointment to Looey's nose as the doctor had instructed him, but after several weeks of treating the nose in this fashion, it became apparent that the lesion was not improving. He therefore scheduled a follow-up visit with Looey's veterinarian to seek further assistance.

Upon reexamining the lesion, his veterinarian still did not feel it was anything serious and prescribed a different topical therapy, instructing Rick to apply this new medication several times a day for one month. If the lesion did not get better he wanted Rick to call him and let him know.

Still not worried about the lesion based upon the veterinarian's reassurance that it wasn't anything to be concerned about, Rick applied this new ointment to Looey's nose as prescribed. One month later the lesion had not only failed to go away, but was actually growing. It now resembled an ulcerative mass that appeared to be destroying the very tip of Looey's right nostril. As he had done twice before, Rick scheduled another follow-up visit with Looey's veterinarian.

During this visit, the veterinarian now suspected that something more serious might be happening to Looey. He thought that the lesion resembled a condition called discoid lupus erythematosus, or DLE, an autoimmune disease that is a benign form of a more serious problem called systemic lupus erythematosus, SLE, or simply lupus. SLE, which occurs in both people and pets, results in the body's immune system attacking the patient's own organs. Even with aggressive immunosuppressive chemotherapy, it can be fatal. DLE, on the other hand, is a more benign form of SLE. When diagnosed and treated early, it usually causes nothing more than a few skin lesions around the face that will go away with the proper treatment.

Confident that Looey's problem was DLE, his veterinarian prescribed a strong immunosuppressive dose of prednisone and instructed Rick to give it to Looey orally twice daily. He told him that side effects of prednisone, which commonly occur at these higher doses, would probably be seen in Looey. They include increased eating, drinking, and urinating. The doctor told

Rick these side effects were not serious and would only last while Looey was on the higher dose of the steroids needed to bring his DLE into remission. Once the dog was in remission and his lesion was resolving, the doctor would lower Looey's dose of steroids to a maintenance dose that should not cause the side effects.

Rick began administering the prescribed dose of prednisone, confident that the true nature of Looey's problem had finally been determined. He was relieved to find out that this condition was not fatal and would quickly resolve after a few weeks of prednisone therapy. Looey took the prednisone without any problems, although he did experience the side effects that the doctor mentioned. These were not serious, although Rick did have to let Looey out to go to the bathroom more often.

As requested, Rick made a follow-up phone call to Looey's veterinarian about two weeks after starting the prednisone therapy, when the doctor expected that the lesion on Looey's right nostril would be much better if not completely gone. Unfortunately, the lesion was still present. Looey's veterinarian assured Rick this was nothing to worry about. While lesions of immune diseases of the skin like DLE usually improve after two weeks of prednisone therapy, some do take longer to cure. The doctor assured Rick that there was nothing to worry about and instructed him to continue the prednisone treatment for another two weeks. At that time, Rick was to make another phone call to report on Looey's condition.

After two more weeks of prednisone therapy, the spot was even larger and more ulcerated. Rick reported this to Looey's doctor, who then decided to increase the dose of prednisone. As the doctor explained, sometimes higher doses of immunosuppressive drugs are needed to treat stubborn cases of immune diseases like DLE.

Rick gave Looey this new higher dose of prednisone for another two weeks. The side effects of the treatment continued, but now Looey started urinating in the house due to the large volume of water he was drinking. Unfortunately, even with this new higher dose of prednisone, the lesion on his nose did not improve and appeared to worsen. At this point, when Rick reported Looey's worsening condition to his veterinarian, the doctor said that he would call a local dermatologist for consultation on this case.

The next day Looey's veterinarian contacted Rick with the results of the consultation. The dermatologist had reviewed Looey's medical records and agreed with his veterinarian that this was nothing more than a particularly tough case of DLE. She prescribed two additional, even stronger immunosuppressive drugs for Looey to take, confident that this new treatment would cure Looey of his DLE.

Unfortunately, after just a few weeks of these new stronger drugs that were supposed to cure him, Looey got very sick. He did not want to eat, was lethargic, and moped around all day, refusing to play or go for his daily walks, and he experienced mild bouts of vomiting and diarrhea. Rick became even more frustrated with these new, obviously more serious side effects of the new drugs. He also noticed that despite all of the different therapies that had been prescribed, the lesion on Looey's nose had grown and was now eating away about a quarter of the front edge of Looey's right nostril.

Rick knew that something was not right and decided to contact the dermatologist on his own, sending her photographs of Looey's nasal lesion. She replied that while this could be something more serious, like a form of nasal cancer, and that a biopsy could be done if he wanted, she still felt that it was simply an aggressive and obviously resistant case of DLE. As such, she recommended working with his local veterinarian to try to find the best dosage of medicines to help Looey without causing the severe side effects he had experienced.

Rick reviewed the dermatologist's recommendations with Looey's original veterinarian. He agreed with the findings, saying that a biopsy could be done but was not necessary and most likely a waste of money, since both doctors thought the problem was nothing more than a bad case of DLE. He encouraged Rick to lower the dose of the strong immunosuppressive medicines in an attempt to prevent side effects, but cautioned Rick that Looey might have to suffer some of the side effects of the medications until the DLE went into remission.

Rick looked very frustrated and appeared to be without much hope for his beloved pet as he related all of this information to me. He had been told for many months that Looey's condition was not serious and should simply get better with medication. Since Looey got sick on his most recent therapy and his nose continued to worsen after trying multiple therapies that Rick had been told should have cured Looey, Rick felt hopeless. The trust he once had in his veterinarian and in the dermatologist had been replaced with fear, doubt, and a strong sense of uncertainty. He didn't want to see his friend suffer, felt that no one could help him, and had given up hope that anyone could find out what was really wrong with Looey.

Fortunately, Rick happened to be shopping at a local health food store a few weeks later. During a discussion with the clerk, Rick mentioned his frustration and feeling of hopelessness regarding Looey's disease. The clerk asked Rick if he had ever thought of taking Looey to a holistic veterinarian for help. Rick took several natural supplements each day for his own health, but he didn't know there were any holistic veterinarians in the area. The clerk, familiar with my practice, gave Rick one of my business cards and encouraged him to bring Looey to our practice.

Before I go into the examining room to greet each owner and pet and begin a visit, my assistant Sandy escorts them into a room to get comfortable while they wait for me. She then brings the chart back to my office and gives me some basic information about the case to better prepare me for the visit.

All of my staff have seen some pretty miraculous healing with the integrative approach to health care. They also appreciate that when a case appears hopeless it may not be so, but when my assistant found me in my office, she had that "it doesn't look good" look on her face. She verbalized her feelings, telling me that this poor dog only had half a nose.

I've seen creatures like this before, with their faces eaten away by some sort of serious infection or aggressive cancer. Those cases have usually progressed so far by the time I see them that there really is very little I can do for most of these pets except keep them very comfortable, prevent further trauma or infection to their sores, and try to slow down the rapid growth of some of these lesions. I knew without even having stepped a foot into the examination room that whatever I was going to face was not going to be easy.

Looey was indeed a pitiful sight to behold. As my assistant had warned me, the right half of his nostril was almost totally gone. The normal black nasal tissue was replaced by a pinkish red, aggressive-looking growth that was eating into his face.

Looey, however, didn't really seem to know that anything was wrong with him. He was quite cheerful and eagerly approached me while waiting for me to pet him on his head. As I do with so many of these big dogs, for whom I hold a special fondness, I immediately accepted his invitation and sat on the floor next to him, petting him on the head and scratching him under his jaw and chest. I knew that I had immediately made a new friend! While I always do my best not to become too personally attached to a pet, I think that the bonding that I do with each patient during my examination compels me to try even harder to find a solution for the pet's problem.

I reviewed all the medical records Rick had brought with him. After reading the notes made on the records by both the original veterinarian and the dermatologist, I was pretty convinced that Looey did not have a case of DLE. I told Rick that I'd never seen so aggressive a lesion associated with what is typically a benign, easy-to-cure, although uncommon, disease. I even went so far as to tell him that I'd never seen a lesion of DLE look this aggressive, in my dermatology textbooks.

Rick somewhat reluctantly indicated that he understood what I was telling him. Despite the fact that deep down I believed that Rick knew Looey was suffering from something more severe, like nasal cancer, he wanted to hold onto the belief that Looey's other doctors were correct in their assessment and that Looey had simply failed to respond to their therapies.

It's always hard to accept a diagnosis of cancer, which is usually ultimately fatal in many pets. Rick had been told so many times by two different doctors that Looey's condition was not a fatal one that I believed it was hard for him to finally accept the reality that they had been wrong in their diagnosis.

I did ask Rick why no one had ever recommended a biopsy of the lesion, especially when it failed to respond to multiple aggressive drugs. He stated that the dermatologist had mentioned the possibility of doing a biopsy in passing, but made it seem like it wasn't necessary since she knew the cause of the lesion.

This was quite frustrating to me. A basic rule of medicine teaches us that if a problem does not get better when the correct therapy is chosen, we must reevaluate our initial impression as it's probably wrong. Any veterinary student could tell that simply giving this dog more drugs was not the way to go. No definitive diagnosis had ever been made; Looey had simply been treated based on an educated guess that was obviously incorrect.

I knew that Looey needed a biopsy to confirm what I suspected. Since Rick was obviously confused and distraught based upon everything that had happened, and expressed some reluctance to putting his dog through a biopsy, I recommended that he and Looey visit one of our local cancer specialists for more help. I warned him that she would also probably recommend a biopsy of the lesion on what remained of Looey's right nostril and asked him to seriously consider getting it done, as this was our only way to know what was really wrong with Looey and how best to treat him.

While I appreciated Rick's hesitation in putting his dog through what is typically a minor surgical procedure, I assured him that Looey was otherwise in good health and should not suffer any ill effects from the biopsy. I told him that I would visit with him and Looey again after his visit to the specialist. Once we had the right diagnosis, I was looking forward to putting together an integrative program to help this special dog.

Fortunately, Rick did take my advice and scheduled an appointment with a local cancer specialist. He couldn't just sit by and watch as his dog's face was being destroyed by whatever was growing on it. The specialist, one of the few cancer specialists in the area who is very supportive of my integrative approach to treating cancer, called me after seeing Looey and Rick. She told me that she was able to talk Rick into allowing her to biopsy Looey's nose. Unfortunately, the result was not good. As I had suspected, it came back as cancer, specifically squamous cell carcinoma, a type of cancer that commonly affects this area of the body. Now I knew for sure why Looey did not respond to any of the aggressive therapies that had been recommended for treating what his other doctors thought was simply a stubborn case of DLE. While his medications should have worked if he actually had DLE, there was no way in the world they would help him recover from this cancer.

The second piece of bad news that the cancer specialist gave me was that there was nothing she could do for Looey. If he was a cat, and if the lesion had been caught very early, radiation therapy might be curative, but aggressive squamous cell carcinoma of the nose in a dog like Looey could not be treated with conventional therapies. She had the unfortunate job of sharing this dismal news with Rick.

When I talked with Rick following my conversation with the specialist, he still maintained his attitude of wanting to do anything he could to help Looey, despite Looey's age and the poor outlook, now that he knew the real cause of the problem. He was especially frustrated at his other doctors and felt like he had wasted a lot of time and money treating the wrong disease. He also felt especially bad for Looey, knowing he had put his dog through all these therapies and their side effects while the cancer was eating away at his face.

I did my best to comfort Rick, letting him know he did the best job with the information he had been given. His only goal was to find relief for Looey, and he was still committed to trying to save his friend. I honestly told him that I didn't have any miracle cures for Looey, but that I would do what I could to make Looey comfortable and to slow down the growth of this aggressive cancer.

First, I reviewed Looey's diet with Rick. Research has shown that diets high in protein and fat, especially omega-3 fatty acids from fish oil, and low in carbohydrates are the best diets to feed pets with cancer. I gave Rick some advice on how to improve Looey's diet to help starve the cancer cells.

I also prescribed high doses of fish oil, rich in omega-3 fatty acids, which have been shown to slow down the growth and spread of cancer, ONCO Support by Rx Vitamins *for* Pets, and Vetri-DMG by Vetri-Science. These potent herbal formulas are very useful in healing pets with any type of cancer.

To help Looey detoxify his body, I prescribed the Detox-Kit

by Heel, a homeopathic detoxification that helps cleanse the body of toxins. Antioxidants are also very useful in slowing the growth of cancer, so I prescribed Super-Ox by Nutri-West.

In addition, I sent Looey home with a special herbal formula that is made for my practice by an herbal pharmacist. It's called Squamous Cell Formula and is used in just these types of cases.

Finally, I had to address topical therapy for Looey's tumor. At this time, the ulcerated lesion eating away at Looey's face was not infected, although I warned Rick that infection was likely at some point in the future and might require both topical and oral antibiotic therapy. To help prevent infection and reduce the inflammation of the tumor, I prescribed Traumeel made by the Heel company. This homeopathic gel is very useful in caring for wounds. While I knew that Looey would ultimately lick off most of the gel, I instructed Rick to apply it as often as he could to Looey's nose. I told him he could alternate that healing gel with any other topical healing preparation he might like to use, such as aloe vera gel or vitamin E oil.

I was frank with Rick and told him that I knew the tumor would grow, continuing to eat away at Looey's face. There was no way to know how much time he had left, as he had valiantly fought this cancer on his own without the correct therapy for over a year before it was properly diagnosed. Rick knew that Looey was living on borrowed time. He hoped, however, that since his pet had lived this long with his cancer without any type of therapy, that the therapies I had chosen for him would continue to strengthen his immune system and keep the cancer in check for as long as possible.

As I write this story, it's been several months since I first diagnosed Looey's cancer. While the tumor continues to grow, Looey acts as if it's not even there. Rick continues to love him and to monitor his cancer, and knows that every day he has with Looey is a special gift. While Rick knows that he will probably have to make the difficult decision for euthanasia at some point in the very near future, his only thoughts now are of spending as much time with this wonderful dog and of celebrating their companionship.

K.C.

As I write about Sadie and Looey, I'm reminded of one of my very first cases involving an owner who went the extra mile for his special older pet. Alfred was one of my most memorable clients. He was an eccentric fellow who was strongly bonded to his twenty-something, very vocal male chocolate point Siamese cat named K.C. I never knew exactly how old K.C. really was, but Alfred told me he was at least twenty. Since Alfred was acutely aware that K.C. was getting toward the end of his life, he never really wanted to think about K.C.'s exact age, feeling that if he thought about it or vocalized his true age, it would put K.C. one step closer to the end of his life.

While I had seen Alfred and K.C. for many years for preventive care, this particular visit was the first and only time I saw K.C. for a medical problem. After gently placing him on his favorite blanket that Alfred carefully laid on my examination table, he pointed out a tiny bump about the size of a green pea located under the skin near the base of K.C.'s tail, where it joined the rest of his body. It took a few moments for Alfred to actually find the bump, as it was quite mobile. Then he held it still for me so that I could examine its size and consistency.

Normally I like to aspirate all lumps and bumps with a tiny needle and syringe, examining the aspirated fluid and cells microscopically to determine the cause of the lump or bump. However, this mass was so tiny that an aspirate was not possible. I told Alfred that the best course of action would be to surgically remove and biopsy the mass. While K.C. was our oldest patient at the time, his recent physical examination and biannual blood testing showed that he was in very good health and had no physical problems that would place him at any greater risk for complications from anesthesia. Also, since I use a holistic approach to anesthesia and would be giving K.C. only enough isoflurane gas to relax him enough to allow me to remove the mass, there would be very little risk indeed. I assured Alfred that K.C. would be carefully monitored during the anesthetic procedure by my assistant and our anesthetic-monitoring machines. I expected the procedure to take no more than fifteen to twenty minutes and told Alfred that he could wait while I did the surgery and then take K.C. home as soon as we were done. Alfred agreed that this was the best course of action and wanted to schedule the surgery as soon as possible.

I had an opening in my surgery schedule for the next day, so I sent Alfred and K.C. home with preoperative fasting instructions and told Alfred to bring K.C. back bright and early at eight o'clock the next morning.

K.C. was my first surgery of the day, and Alfred was already waiting patiently at the door when I arrived. It took just a few minutes to have Alfred sign his surgical authorization forms and have my assistant prep K.C. for his surgery. The entire procedure took only twenty minutes from start to finish, and K.C. recovered from his anesthesia quite well. He was discharged about ten minutes after he woke up from the anesthetic gas. As I was reviewing the discharge instructions with Alfred, I told him I expected to have the results of K.C.'s biopsy within two to three days and would call him as soon as the results came in. Alfred wrapped K.C. up in his favorite blanket and carefully carried him from our office, gently placing him on the passenger seat of his car to begin the trip home.

A few days later, the pathology laboratory faxed K.C.'s biopsy results. While I was hoping it would simply be a cyst or a fatty tumor, it actually came back as a kind of cancer called a fibrosarcoma. These tumors are among the most common cancers that occur under the skin of cats. There are several subsets of fibrosarcomas, but most have been linked to the chronic inflammation that we often see with repeated vaccination. As a result of the increased incidence of these types of tumors, and the knowledge that pets build up long-lasting immunity to vaccinations, annual vaccinations are no longer recommended and are in fact discouraged.

I called Alfred with the news that K.C. unfortunately had cancer. While we now have many good conventional therapies, including surgery, chemotherapy, and radiation therapy, to help cats with fibrosarcoma live a long time before their cancer returns, at the time of K.C.'s diagnosis the only conventional care I could offer him was the surgical removal of his tumor I had just done. I explained to Alfred that even though I felt that I removed the entire tiny tumor, fibrosarcomas are aggressive cancers that recur despite what appears to be complete surgical removal.

While my array of alternative therapies has increased dramatically since I saw K.C. many years ago, at that time I had very little I could offer him. However, a natural product was available by injection that was reported to slow down the growth of solid tumors like fibrosarcomas. This product was marketed under the name Acemannan, and was essentially a potent extract of the aloe vera plant, long recognized for its healing properties. Alfred wanted to do anything possible to have K.C. live forever, and readily agreed to try the Acemannan therapy. I told Alfred that the protocol involved injecting the Acemannan into K.C.'s body and also into the area where the tumor had been removed. I scheduled a number of follow-up appointments for K.C. to receive his series of injections.

K.C. tolerated the Acemannan therapy without any side effects, as I had expected. Unfortunately, a few months following his initial surgery, the fibrosarcoma tumor returned in its original location. Since cost was not a factor for Alfred, he quickly scheduled a second surgery for his beloved K.C. That surgery also went off without a hitch, and we restarted the Acemannan therapy as soon as K.C. recovered from the surgery.

For the next year, K.C. would undergo several more surgeries and Acemannan therapies as the tumor recurred every few months. Still, Alfred was happy to do whatever we needed to do to keep K.C.'s cancer from growing and spreading. If there was anything that could be done to fight K.C.'s cancer, Alfred readily agreed to do it.

Of course, we can only cheat death for so long. I would love to report that K.C. is still alive and pushing thirty-five years old. That would certainly make him the oldest living cat on record, K.C. did finally pass away about two years after his first surgery to remove his fibrosarcoma tumor. The good news is that his cancer was not the cause of death. Kidney failure, a common disease that afflicts and kills many older cats and dogs, was his downfall.

Still, this case shows us that no pet is "too old" for therapy. With owners like Alfred, who are committed to keeping their pets healthy and living as long as possible, and for whom the cost of care is not an issue, an integrative approach can offer our older dogs and cats many good years of health and happiness.

What about those cases where cost is a factor, or the pet's age precludes the most aggressive therapy possible even if the owner can afford it? Integrative medicine offers these pets and their owners a lot as well. The following case is very typical of the healing power of integrative medicine.

Jack

Jack was an older yellow Labrador retriever. At age fifteen, he actually held the record for being the oldest Labrador in our practice. His longevity was attributed to good breeding, a great diet, judicious use of nutritional supplements to keep him healthy throughout his life, and an aggressive preventive-care program put in place by his owners, Maria and Richard.

Jack had been a patient of mine since he was a young puppy,

and I had the pleasure of watching him grow into a wonderful adult male retriever. I remember fondly Maria and Richard sharing stories of Jack's antics with me. They showed me pictures of him jumping off the diving board of their swimming pool, shooting to the bottom of the pool to retrieve Frisbees that they threw into the water. Like most Labradors, Jack loved the water. He would spend long periods of time retrieving Frisbees and other objects from the bottom of their pool. He loved to go for long walks and play fetch with his favorite tennis ball, and was a very active and healthy dog.

Fortunately, he was not afflicted with any of the problems that typically affect retrievers, like allergies, chronic skin infections, and chronic ear infections. I rarely saw Jack for medical issues, instead visiting with him only twice each year as he came in for his semiannual physical examinations and blood and urine testing.

In his younger days, Jack, while a very sweet dog, always resisted having his blood drawn. I have very vivid memories of Maria, Richard, and my entire staff trying to hold Jack still while I drew the small amount of blood that was necessary for his laboratory evaluation. Due to the strength that he exhibited while being restrained, I often would have to draw blood out of several veins in order to get enough to run the tests I needed. What should normally take all of one or two minutes quickly turned into a five-to-ten minute procedure, inevitably tiring out all of us, except of course Jack, who was just warming up!

Now that Jack was the most senior canine citizen in my practice, he started to exhibit more of the medical problems that are commonly seen in older pets. Fortunately, as he advanced in age he also had mellowed out when we had to draw blood from him.

Usually Richard could hold him still for me while one of my assistants held his leg so that I could draw blood from his vein, with Maria gently rubbing Jack's head, speaking to him softly to relax him. Thankfully, my entire staff was not needed to restrain Jack anymore.

Most of Jack's geriatric medical issues were not too serious. As a younger dog, I had removed several fatty tumors from his body. Jack was not a cooperative patient postoperatively, however, and always managed to chew his sutures out, which meant that invariably I had to resew his incision at least once. We tried applying Elizabethan collars to prevent him from reaching the incisions, but he did not tolerate these collars and always found a way to remove them from his head and to destroy them so that he could once again resume chewing out his sutures, necessitating follow-up surgeries to repair the incisions. Now that Jack was getting older he had developed a few more fatty tumors. While cost was never a factor with Richard and Maria, they made the decision not to have me remove these additional tumors. Their rationale, which made a lot of sense to me, was that since the tumors were not bothering Jack and were not cancerous, they were better left alone so that Richard and Maria would not have to deal with the trauma of Jack interfering with the healing process that was necessary if they were removed surgically.

Like many older large breeds of dogs, Jack did develop arthritis of his hips and spine. Wanting to avoid using conventional medications with their possible side effects for as long as possible, Richard and Maria administered several joint supplements to Jack. These kept him very comfortable and allowed him to still enjoy his walks and playtime with them. While Jack was certainly a good candidate for a total hip replacement, a procedure in which new hip joints are made for the dog, Richard and Maria agreed with me that since Jack had already exceeded the life expectancy for a Labrador retriever, our main goal should be keeping him comfortable as he continued to age gracefully.

Finally, and perhaps most important, Jack developed a tiny pink growth just inside the opening of his left nostril. When his owners pointed this out to me during one of their recent visits, I told them that a biopsy of the lesion would be best so that we would know if this was anything of concern. We discussed the likelihood that this could be a benign nasal polyp or wart, or even something more serious such as a small cancerous growth affecting his nose. Richard and Maria were realistic. They made it clear that due to Jack's age they would not pursue aggressive therapies like chemotherapy or radiation if the growth turned out to be cancer. They did want to get the lesion removed from his nose, however, as it did make Jack sneeze and occasionally caused a nosebleed.

I explained to them that my goal is to always recommend what is best for each pet, without regard to the cost of therapy, as only each owner knows what is affordable. While I don't let the pet's age influence my recommendation, I'm also very realistic. For a dog like Jack, who had already outlived his life expectancy, aggressive therapies are not necessarily indicated or in his best interest. Still, it is up to each owner to determine the best course of action, taking into account the pet's current health and age, the cost of therapy, and the pet's ability to cooperate with whatever therapy is chosen. I agreed with Richard and Maria that we should do everything possible to keep Jack comfortable, but not go overboard and place too much stress on him. Jack had experienced a wonderful life, having been spoiled for fifteen years by his owners. His life up to this point had been a very healthy one, and even if the tiny lesion in his nostril was cancer, I felt comfortable that Jack would die of old age long before the cancer would kill him.

Richard and Maria appreciated my honesty as well as my desire to respect their wishes regarding Jack's care. They did accept my referral to our local cancer specialist, who was able to totally remove and biopsy the pink growth in Jack's left nostril. Unfortunately, the biopsy did reveal cancer. The specialist discussed radiation therapy with Richard and Maria, but they declined this treatment due to Jack's age and concerns over his quality of life. As I discussed with them after their visit to the specialist, radiation therapy is very effective in controlling tumors like the one Jack had, but I reiterated that it probably would not make a difference for Jack, since he was already living on borrowed time even though he did not know it.

To keep Jack comfortable and to try to slow down the regrowth of his nasal cancer, I prescribed the drug piroxicam. This potent medication, a nonsteroidal drug, is often used to slow down the growth and spread of cancers in pets. Coincidentally, it provides pain relief for pets with arthritis, so I knew it could also help Jack with his hip and back issues.

Supplements that I chose to help him fight his cancer included the antioxidant Proanthozone by Animal Health Options, ONCO Support by Rx Vitamins *for* Pets, and Ultra EFA, a potent fatty acid also made by this company.

To date, Jack is doing wonderfully, and is now very calm when we draw his blood. His nasal tumor has not returned since its first appearance over one year ago. He's taking all of his supplements, is not experiencing any side effects from his piroxicam therapy, and still has a lot of youthful energy in his fifteen-year-old body. While he has lost a lot of weight, mainly muscle mass, over the past few years, he still is enjoying life and seems content with the world around him.

Richard and Maria discussed with me the fact that while Jack appears to be in good health and spirits, they know that he won't be around forever. They are already making plans for what to do with him when he dies, and are checking into the services offered by some of our local pet cemeteries. They're not morbid about this, but instead are doing it while Jack is healthy and they are not affected by the grief that will inevitably come with his passing. Their approach to his end-of-life care is very normal and makes a lot of sense. While not going overboard with aggressive therapies, there's no question that they're doing the best job for Jack and are ensuring that however much time he has remaining will be good quality time that they and Jack will all enjoy.

The integrative approach to health care is especially well suited for our geriatric population. Each pet and each situation is unique, and there is no cookie-cutter approach in deciding the best options. These special pets and their adoring owners require special care. Modern medicine can no longer take the attitude that the geriatric population is expendable or that treatment should not be given simply because the patient is too old. Instead, health-care professionals must embrace life at every stage, from womb to tomb, from cradle to grave. By working with the pets' owners and discussing rational therapeutic options, a treatment plan can be devised for every situation. Doing so allows us to embrace end-of-life issues with dignity and helps ensure the pet will enjoy whatever time it has left with a good quality of life. Family members don't give up on a pet simply because the pet is old, and neither should its doctors.

12

Sometimes I Feel Hopeless

So far, all of the cases I've shared with you involve situations where conventional medicine was not able to help these special patients. While these cases are often frustrating for the pet owner as well as myself and my staff, some are especially frustrating. These are the cases where I know that I can help the pet but the owner won't let me. Especially depressing are situations where a few simple steps could prevent the unnecessary suffering and the untimely death of my patient.

Frisky

Frisky was a six-year-old neutered West Highland white terrier. Like all Westies, he was a happy and hearty little soul until he was stricken with lymphosarcoma, a cancer of the lymphatic system. While no cancer is really "good" to have, if I had to give a pet cancer, it would probably be lymphosarcoma, because this type is usually very responsive to conventional chemotherapy drugs. Most pets respond very well to chemotherapy and can easily live twelve months or more before the cancer comes out of remission. When I use an integrative approach, adding supplements to the traditional chemotherapy protocol, many of my patients live quite a bit longer, rarely suffer from any side effects, and generally feel great while they're battling their cancer. The good news about using chemotherapy drugs in pets is that, unlike the situation commonly encountered when people are treated with these drugs, most pets have few if any side effects. When I use my nutritional, herbal, and homeopathic supplements along with the chemotherapy, side effects are even rarer and the chemotherapy works much better in killing the cancer. When this integrative approach is used, my patients just do better and live longer.

Consequently, when I visited with Frisky's owners, Bob and Tina, and reviewed Frisky's medical records, I was excited that I would be able to offer their pet a good prognosis despite the fact that he would most likely one day die from his lymphosarcoma cancer. I also reviewed the laboratory findings they brought with them, and was happy to see that his blood and urine testing did not detect any problems resulting from his cancer that were affecting any of his other organs. It was obvious that Frisky was an otherwise healthy pet that simply needed help battling his cancer. I told Bob and Tina that while there are never any guarantees, based upon my years of experience in healing many pets with this type of cancer, I thought Frisky should do very well and hopefully live one, two, or even several more years.

I could tell by observing him that Frisky was not the normal, happy little Westie that I expect to see when this breed of dog comes into my office. Even though all of his laboratory values were normal, I knew that his cancer was zapping his energy, something that often happens when cancer is initially diagnosed in dogs and cats. Since no treatment of any kind had been started, I knew that I had to do something to immediately make him feel better so that other therapies could work to their full extent.

I reviewed with Bob and Tina all of the different treatment options that were available to help dogs afflicted with lymphosarcoma. I also told them that I liked thinking of chemotherapy as a "quick kill" for cancer, one that puts the pet into remission and helps it feel better. Then various herbs, homeopathics, and other nutritional therapies are used to support the pet's organs and strengthen its immune system to keep the remaining cancerous cells in remission for as long as possible.

Unfortunately, Bob and Tina would have none of this. They were totally opposed to chemotherapy even after I tried to convince them that it was unlikely that Frisky would suffer any ill effects from the drugs used to kill his lymphosarcoma. They also declined a referral to a cancer specialist who could provide further information and answers to their concerns. This seemed more than a bit strange to me. Here I was, offering them a chance to save their pet's life, and yet they kept declining my recommendations. It just didn't make any sense.

Shortly after rejecting my treatment recommendations for chemotherapy, Bob explained their decision. In the past year, he had suffered from prostate cancer and had gone through chemotherapy, which he said was the worst experience of his life. He felt deathly ill from his chemotherapy treatment, at one point even praying for death, and would never put his dog through that. He even went so far as to tell me that if his prostate cancer ever came back, he would let it run its course and kill him rather than go through another round of chemo.

I knew I would have a tough time trying to convince Bob and Tina that chemotherapy was essential in trying to give Frisky the best chance at living more than a few months. Without it, I knew it was unlikely that my alternative treatments would do much for him. While I've had many cases, a few of which I've shared throughout this book, that did very well with only alternative therapies, I also knew from experience that the best therapy for healing a pet with cancer involves doing everything, including chemotherapy, when at all possible. The more we can do to kill the cancer, the greater the likelihood that the pet will live longer and possibly even be cured of the cancer.

Again I tried to assure Bob and Tina that his unfortunate experience, while common in many people treated with chemotherapy, was very uncommon in pets. Furthermore, the supplements I would prescribe for Frisky would maximize the effectiveness of the chemotherapy drugs while minimizing their side effects. I further reiterated that with all of the experience I had in treating pets with chemotherapy for over fifteen years, I could count on one hand the number of pets who ever showed any side effects. (Because many pet owners still have horrible misconceptions about the use of chemotherapy in pets, I've since written a book to address these concerns, *The Natural Vet's Guide to Preventing and Treating Cancer in Dogs*.)

Still Bob and Tina wouldn't budge from their "no chemo" attitude. While I still believe in doing anything possible to help my patients, and have had several miraculous healings of pets with very aggressive cancers that were not treated with chemotherapy, I had to be honest with them. I told them that most pets treated only with supplements did not do as well as pets prescribed supplements integrated with conventional therapies like chemotherapy.

At the time of this visit, I had only been treating pets with cancer for a short time. I did not have nearly the experience or the vast array of supplements to help my cancer patients that I have now. Consequently, I told them that if we only did supplementation, I could not guarantee them the good results I would expect to see if we also used chemotherapy.

My numerous attempts to get them to change their minds were futile. They just didn't want any chemotherapy for their pet and were convinced that an alternative approach, using only natural therapies, would cure their little dog.

Desperate to help Frisky, I made one final plea. I asked them if they would consent to letting me use prednisone as part of my therapy. Prednisone is one of several chemotherapy drugs that can be quite helpful for pets with various cancers such as lymphosarcoma. By itself, it usually only puts a pet into remission for a few months. Still, I hoped that by combining prednisone with the few supplements I had available at my disposal at that time, I would be able to help Frisky live a little bit longer than if I only prescribed the supplements.

Once again they refused; absolutely no drugs were to be used to try to help their pet. Based upon Bob's horrible experience with his chemotherapy, they refused to listen to logic and budge from their convictions, insisting that Frisky would suffer immensely if we used any conventional medications in trying to help him heal from his cancer.

Knowing my arguments were falling on deaf ears, I reluctantly relented. Deep down inside, I knew that it was extremely unlikely that Frisky would be with us much longer and would probably suffer from his cancer until Bob and Tina made the decision for euthanasia. Two weeks later, I was proved correct. Despite using the supplements I had prescribed, but at no surprise to me, Frisky deteriorated quickly. His lymph nodes under his jaw had doubled in size, causing him pain when he tried to eat or drink. The cancer was overwhelming his system and his entire day consisted of lying around as he was too weak and sick to interact with Bob and Tina. His owners made an appointment for the following day to end Frisky's suffering. I ended Frisky's life that bright sunny Wednesday afternoon in March, knowing it was the best thing for him to end the suffering he experienced from his spreading cancer, but it was a euthanasia that should not have occurred so soon after his diagnosis. If only Bob and Tina had been open to hearing the facts I repeatedly gave to them during their visit, I know that Frisky could have lived pain free for quite some time. While I don't like to second-guess owners' decisions, I do become frustrated when a wrong decision has a tragic ending. It's bad enough when I lose a patient because a disease ultimately wins. Even when that death is expected, it still hurts.

It's a horrible feeling when I lose a patient I know I could have saved. While I know that Bob and Tina felt they made the right decision, it was made based on emotion and misinformation, and it resulted in the untimely and totally unnecessary death of a fine animal. Frisky became the first of my memorable cases whose life ended way before it should have. Unfortunately there would be more.

One of my five goals for a holistic health-care program is to prevent disease. It's always much better and usually much less expensive to prevent a problem than to treat it. Another goal is to help the owner decrease the cost of pet care without cutting corners that might place the pet's health or life at risk, and to meet that goal, my staff and I constantly brainstorm and try to create preventive-care programs. These programs are designed to allow us to detect disease in a pet before it becomes ill, at a greatly reduced cost to the pet owner.

One of my favorite preventive-care programs is called our Health Profile. This profile, done when the patient is under anesthesia for another procedure such as a dental cleaning, a tumor removal, or even a spaying or neutering, includes an EKG to screen for cardiac diseases, and radiographs of the pet's chest and abdomen, looking for abnormalities like tumors or abscesses. The full cost of an EKG or radiograph would normally be around two hundred to three hundred dollars. When the Health Profile is done during another procedure, the reduced cost is only fifty dollars! This has allowed us to detect some pretty serious problems, including bladder stones and cancers, in pets that otherwise appeared healthy.

Ginger

Ginger, a seven-year-old beautiful yellow Labrador retriever-mix, was one patient for whom my receptionist recommended a Health Profile when she was brought in for her dental cleaning. At the time of her visit, the Health Profile was one of several optional procedures an owner could select to have done while the pet was asleep, but because of what happened to Ginger, the Health Profile is no longer optional. Instead, it is now a standard procedure for all of our patients who are anesthetized. Findings from the Health Profile have allowed us to save the lives of many of our special patients by detecting hidden problems before the pets became ill.

Unfortunately, Ginger's owner, Marie, was never one to spend money on any additional optional procedures, even if they were greatly reduced in price. While I was happy that Marie at least consented to a dental cleaning (after much prodding from me over the years), she was typical of the owner who only wanted "minimal care" for her pet. While I understand that cost is always a factor, responsible pet ownership does require spending some money to keep the pet healthy. We do as much as we can in our practice to decrease the cost of care and work with pet owners who are on a very strict budget. I'm a big fan of certain pet insurance policies that can really decrease the cost of care, even basic maintenance like dental cleanings. My staff and I really have a hard time when owners decline procedures such as our Health Profile. For only fifty more dollars, owners get a lot of information about their pets' health, and sometimes this information can be lifesaving.

Since Marie had been bringing Ginger to my practice for many years, I knew that she was always concerned about cost. She made it clear each and every visit that she didn't want to spend much money, even though she "dearly loved Ginger and would do anything for her." After doing the least amount of care possible at every office visit, complaining about the cost at the end of every office visit, Marie would take Ginger home, driving off in the newest-model luxury car! Therefore, I was not at all surprised when reviewing her signed anesthesia authorization form to see that Marie had declined all of the optional procedures we offered, including the reduced-priced Health Profile.

Fortunately, Ginger's dental procedure went well that morning, and she was discharged, shortly before noon. Marie was very thankful that Ginger did well with her anesthesia, commenting on her lovely teeth and fresh breath, and when she paid her bill, once again commented on "how much it costs to own a dog." She then loaded Ginger into her new, shiny, silver Lexus sedan, a Christmas gift from her executive husband, and drove off. I left for lunch, driving away in my seven-year-old light blue minivan, its right-side sliding passenger door slightly damaged from a recent run-in with our sliding wooden gate.

Approximately four months later, Marie was waiting outside our office in her Lexus sedan when we arrived to open for the day. She was quite distressed, as I could tell by her red eyes, puffy eyelids, and tear-streaked face that caused her mascara to run down toward the corners of her lips. She had just picked up Ginger from our local animal emergency room, where Ginger had spent the previous night. This sweet pet, who just four months ago bounded energetically into the waiting room for her dental cleaning, appeared lifeless as we carried her limp and weakened body from Marie's car, gently laying her on our blanketed examination-room table. It was obvious that Ginger was dying, but what had happened to her? What made her take a turn for the worse, when just a few months ago we had cleaned her teeth without any problems?

Marie showed me the medical records from Ginger's night at the emergency room, including the radiographs that the ER doctor had taken of her chest and abdomen. Ginger's problem was immediately obvious. She had a huge bladder stone in her abdomen. Normally these stones reside in the urinary bladder, where they often do not cause problems until they grow in size. Even asymptomatic stones should be removed in most pets, however, as they can grow or cause discomfort to the pet or create a blockage of the urinary system.

In Ginger's case, a single large stone, about the size of a silver dollar, was located in Ginger's abdominal cavity, outside of its normal location in the urinary bladder. The stone was so large that it had ruptured Ginger's bladder, causing it to leak urine into her abdominal cavity, resulting in severe peritonitis. This is a very, very painful condition for pets, and requires emergency surgery to treat. Even with early diagnosis and surgery, the mortality rate is high. Nevertheless, surgery had not been performed at the emergency clinic the previous night, when it should have been done, and I guessed that was due to the cost of the procedure. Careful questioning of Marie revealed that was indeed a factor. Marie told me that while she would "do anything to help Ginger," she felt it was best that I perform euthanasia. After reviewing the records, and seeing the amount of suffering Ginger was experiencing, I agreed to quickly, painlessly, and humanely end the life of this beautiful creature.

This was indeed a tragic case. Even though she was a larger breed of dog, Ginger was only seven years old, barely past middle age. She should not have died so young, and her death was totally preventable. For a mere fifty dollars, the cost of our optional Health Profile, a simple radiograph of her abdomen taken during her dental cleaning four months prior to her untimely demise would have easily revealed her large bladder stone, still located inside her urinary bladder. It then could have been removed safely and quickly, preventing the eventual rupture of her bladder and unnecessary death.

Saving money on pet care is a noble goal, but putting a pet's health and life at risk to save fifty dollars makes absolutely no sense to me. I hate losing any patient, but I really hate losing a patient whose death was totally preventable. I can offer a lot of hope for my patients by using integrative therapies, but owners have to do their part. Unfortunately, failure to spend a little money in order to allow early detection of a disease would become a theme in the unnecessary death of another special pet a few years later.

Champp

Champ was owned by Bill and Elizabeth, a middle-aged couple who first adopted him from the local animal shelter when he was still a puppy. I saw Champ, a cute little bundle of black, wiry hair that totally obscured his small frame, shortly after Bill and Elizabeth brought him home from the shelter. I watched Champ grow over the years from that tiny bundle of black fur into a fifty-pound, good-looking mature terrier-mix dog. I also watched as his owners started having children shortly after adopting Champ.

While it was obvious that Bill and Elizabeth were attached to Champ, they left no doubt that he was "just a dog," and they didn't believe in spending a lot of money on his care. Their annual visits with us were erratic. Instead of coming in regularly every twelve months for his annual checkup, sometimes the interval between visits extended to as long as fifteen months or longer. Some years they skipped the required annual visits altogether and only brought Champ in when he had a medical problem, such as a skin infection or irritation of his ears. During these visits, they would usually consent and let me bring Champ up to date with some of his necessary annual care, but they declined his preventive blood and urine testing. Despite needing to have his teeth cleaned for several years due to advancing and painful periodontal disease, they never agreed to a professional cleaning, reminding me once again that Champ was "just a dog." (In my mind, I sarcastically admitted that Champ was "just a dog," but one who continued to suffer from severe periodontal disease and a lack of required preventive health care.)

As Champ grew older, we began sending Bill and Elizabeth reminders so that we could see Champ twice yearly for his preventive care. During these visits, I perform a complete physical examination, blood testing, and a urinalysis to screen for problems like kidney disease, liver disease, and diabetes, plus a fecal analysis to check for parasites, including some that could be transmitted to Bill, Elizabeth, or their young children. Of course, since Champ was "just a dog," I did not see him twice yearly or even yearly for his annual visits.

His most recent visit occurred six months prior to the time he became ill. At that visit, Bill wanted me to check Champ's right ear, which seemed to be bothering him. During my examination, I diagnosed a yeast infection of his right ear and prescribed the appropriate natural ear drops and a few supplements to treat the infection. Although I recommended that we go ahead and collect blood and urine for his annual checkup, I was not at all surprised when Bill declined this additional, necessary preventive care, or when he refused the supplements to treat Champ's ear, taking only the ear drops instead.

Six months later, I saw Champ for the last time, when Bill and Elizabeth brought him to our office, carrying him through our front door as Champ was too weak to walk. We quickly moved Champ back to our treatment room and into one of our hospitalization units. The history they gave me indicated that Champ had begun feeling bad a few days earlier. He would only eat a small amount of "people" food, as he refused his regular dog food, and only if Bill or Elizabeth fed it to him by hand. Champ also drank a very large amount of water that caused him to urinate a lot, often where he was lying, as he was too weak to get up and go outside. Twelve hours prior to bringing him to our office as an emergency visit that Friday morning, Champ had begun throwing up even though he was barely eating anything.

I told Bill and Elizabeth that Champ, who was now eight years old, had clinical signs that were quite nonspecific and common with just about every disease that I see in practice. As a result, my goal that day was to stabilize him with fluid therapy and intravenous vitamins, administer medication and supplements to control his vomiting if it continued, and get blood and urine for laboratory evaluation, in an attempt to give them answers as to the cause of Champ's recent illness. Bill and Elizabeth agreed to my estimate of charges for hospitalizing Champ for the day, attempting to find out what was wrong with him, and helping him recover, if possible.

Champ tolerated his hospitalization quite well. Despite intensive treatment, however, he really didn't look any better when I discharged him later that day. Fortunately, he was also not any worse, so I knew my therapies had at least stabilized his condition for the day. I told Bill and Elizabeth that he would be best served by spending that Friday night and maybe even the entire weekend at the local animal emergency clinic, where doctors could continue to help him recover from whatever was making him sick. Since Bill and Elizabeth had already spent four hundred dollars on Friday's visit, neither my staff nor I was surprised that they elected to take Champ home to see how he did over the weekend. I knew that was the wrong decision, as Champ was very ill and might not even respond to more intensive therapy at the emergency clinic.

Like so many decisions Bill and Elizabeth had made in the

past regarding Champ's health care, I knew I would never be able to change their minds. Some pets can and should continue their healing care at home, but pets as sick as Champ, who showed no signs of improvement despite a day of intensive therapy, really need ongoing care in a veterinary hospital. As Bill and Elizabeth carried a very weak Champ out to their car, I had a sick feeling that I was saying good-bye to him for the last time.

I didn't have to wait long to find out how Champ fared over the weekend. Bill left a message on our office voicemail before we arrived at work Monday morning, thanking us for all that we did for Champ, and told us that he had died at home in his sleep Saturday night.

Bill's voicemail message was not the only thing waiting for me when I arrived at work early that Monday morning. There was also a fax from our local veterinary diagnostic laboratory waiting for me. It contained the results of Champ's blood profile and urinalysis. As I scanned the values on the report, the cause of Champ's sudden illness and subsequent death was readily apparent: severe, chronic, end-stage kidney failure. The values for his kidney enzymes were among the worst that I had seen in over twenty years of practice, which revealed to me just how hopeless Champ's condition was when I saw him. While integrative therapies can help extend the lives of pets with chronic kidney failure, these therapies only work when we intervene at the earliest stages of kidney failure. No matter how well an integrative approach to health care works, integrative therapies can't usually save dying pets like Champ.

Integrative therapies do work very well, however, when started prior to an end-stage condition like the one that affected

Champ. As I shared with my staff, already upset at the loss of this nice dog who had been with our practice since he was a tiny puppy, Champ's death, like Ginger's, was totally preventable. Had Bill agreed to my recommendation to collect samples of blood and urine for laboratory evaluation during Champ's visit with me for his ear infection six months prior to his untimely death, I would have easily diagnosed the beginning stage of Champ's kidney condition. At that point, I could have quickly and effectively intervened and prescribed a number of natural therapies to keep Champ's kidneys from failing for many years. The knowledge we had that Monday morning that we could have prevented yet another totally unnecessary death added to our anguish over the loss of Champ.

The only good news I can find in the tragic and unfortunate deaths of pets like Champ, Frisky, and Ginger is the realization that my staff gains a greater knowledge of and respect for preventive health care. By seeing what can happen when a pet owner declines my recommendations for this care, the staff becomes strengthened in their own belief in the value of these preventive-care recommendations. As they deal with more pet owners down the road, they are better prepared to reinforce my recommendations, which are designed to keep my patients healthy and living for as long as possible.

These deaths are senseless and tragic for a variety of reasons. While I appreciate that every pet owner has a limited budget for pet care, I'm overwhelmed and often left speechless at how little value some people place on their pets, spending money on an expensive car that can't return love and affection rather than on a furry friend, little or big, that will be their constant companion, truly leaves me at a loss for words. It's hard for me to understand a value system that places an inanimate object over a living, breathing, loving creature. Saying "he's only a dog" or "she's only a cat" demeans the value that most of us in society place on our canine and feline family members. It also demeans what I do. If the pet you brought into my office is only a pet, then you really don't need my help. I didn't give up many years of my life struggling to complete a rigorous education in veterinary medicine so that I could be able to offer a pet the best care possible only to have someone to place so little value on it. When I value and care for a pet more than the owner does something is tragically wrong, and I am truly disheartened. As for those pet owners who have children who count on mom and dad to do everything possible to save the family dog or cat, who is often a source of constant joy, pleasure, and love, I consider it especially tragic when parents teach their children, by their actions, that life has so little meaning.

While I don't *blame* pet owners for their decisions, I do *hold them responsible* for their decisions, just as I expect them to hold me responsible for mine. Veterinary medicine has advanced a lot since I first fell in love with this noble and extremely rewarding profession as a teenager in junior high school. Our advanced technologies for diagnosing and treating pets are amazing, but they do come at a cost. Preventive care programs seek to keep pets healthy and allow us to treat diseases before they become fatal, along with the judicious use of discounted health-care programs (like my Health Profile), and, in addition, pet health insurance can keep costs low for owners without jeopardizing the health or life of their pets. By educating pet owners and helping them make the best health-care decisions for their pets, we can avoid unnecessary and tragic deaths like those that befell Frisky, Ginger, and Champ, three marvelous animals who didn't need to die prematurely. Starting on a preventative course when pets are young and maintaining their immune systems throughout their lives will result in fewer hopeless cases, and that is what we all, both pet owners and their doctors, want for our beloved four-legged family members.

Epilogue

All of the patients depicted in this book are real, as are their diseases and treatments. The names of the pets and their owners have been changed to protect medical confidentiality. Most of the patients have responded very well to their integrative therapies. Some, obviously, have passed away due to time or the inevitable consequences of a fatal disease. Owners depicted in *Unexpected Miracles* are grateful for the chance to have offered their pets hope, sometimes against overwhelming odds.

There are never guarantees in life. Still, most pets with illnesses that appear hopeless may be helped and even saved if the right doctor is found and if the correct therapy is used early in the course of the disease. Better yet, starting a pet, and all family members, on a holistic preventive health-care program will do a lot to maximize health and minimize disease. A sound diet, reasonable exercise, proper use of supplements, and judicious use of conventional medications (only when necessary) are the foundations of a holistic, integrative health-care program.

For help in finding a holistic doctor near you, visit www .altvetmed.org.

To keep up with the latest in holistic healing, visit my Web site at www.petcarenaturally.com.

Appendix A

Vaccination Concerns

Throughout the book I discourage the routine use of vaccinations. Current research shows us that pets are capable of forming long-lasting immunity to today's vaccinations. A number of conventional veterinary experts, including the American Veterinary Medical Association, now recommend reducing the frequency with which pets are vaccinated. Current guidelines call for vaccinating most pets every three years, rather than every six to twelve months.

Holistic veterinarians recognize that most pets only need to be vaccinated a few times during their entire lives. Therefore, we recommend the use of an annual blood test called a vaccine titer or antibody test. In my own practice, the results of this test support my belief that vaccines can produce immunity that lasts many years, and in some cases even for the life of the pet.

Unfortunately, many veterinarians still have not changed their vaccination protocols, and continue to vaccinate pets every six to twelve months. Additionally, many grooming and boarding facilities require that pets be vaccinated according to their own specific vaccination protocols, which vary from facility to facility.

I'm often asked by pet owners, "What should I do if I want to board my pets or get them groomed since I don't want to vaccinate my pets more than necessary?"

In these instances, there are only a few options available to the concerned pet owner who wants to practice an integrative approach to health care. I encourage them to talk with their regular veterinarians, boarding facilities, or groomers and inquire if the results of titer testing will be accepted. If the answer is yes, there is no problem. If the answer is no, either the owner can give the pet unnecessary vaccinations or search for a new facility for where vaccine titer testing results will be accepted.

For owners who are a bit bold and not afraid to question authority, I encourage them to ask the person who requires frequent vaccinations and refuses to accept titer testing the following question: "I want to do what's best for my pet but I'm concerned about all the vaccinations you require. Where is the research that shows us that pets need to be vaccinated every six to twelve months?"

Of course, there is *no* research that has ever been done that proves pets need vaccinations as often as many veterinarians do them. Instead the current research shows that pets do *not* need frequent vaccinations.

Finally, the issue of rabies vaccination often comes up. To my knowledge, rabies is the only vaccine that is required by law, generally required every three years. In some states, such as my state of Texas, veterinarians, boarding facilities, and grooming places can require rabies vaccinations every one to three years. *However, there is no difference between a one-year rabies vaccine and a three-year rabies vaccine. They are the exact same vaccine; only the labels are different.* Therefore, I encourage all pets to be vaccinated every three years for rabies rather than annually.

I have mentioned throughout this book that sick pets, older pets, and pets with chronic diseases such as cancer should never receive another vaccine, including a rabies vaccine. *Pets with chronic medical conditions may have their conditions worsened or their cancers come out of remission if they receive a vaccine.* This obviously violates state rabies law.

While I do not encourage people to break the law, as a veterinarian I must recommend what's best for the pet's health. I encourage readers to work with their veterinarians to do what's in their pets' best interests while complying with the law to the best of their ability.

Appendix B

Supplements

Throughout *Unexpected Miracles*, I have mentioned a number of nutritional supplements and therapies that have helped heal my patients. Some of these supplements are available only to veterinarians, others are available only through my practice (as they're made specifically for my patients), and still others are available to any pet owner. I've compiled a list of supplement manufacturers and invite you to contact them for more information on any of the supplements you've read about in this book. I also encourage you to visit my Web site, www .petcarenaturally.com, for links to many of these supplement manufacturers.

Dr. Shawn's Pet Organics
www.DrShawnspetorganics.com
2145 W Park Blvd.
Plano, TX 75075
(972) 867-8800
(877) 929-1515

Rx Vitamins *for* Pets
www.rxvitamins.com
150 Clearbrook Road
Suite 149
Elmsford, NY 10523
(914) 592-2323
(800) 792-2222

Vetri-Science
www.vetriscience.com
U.S. Inquiries (800) 882-9993

Nutri-West
www.nutriwest.com
P.O. Box 950
Douglas, WY 82633
(307) 358-5066
(800) 443-3333

Evergreen Herbs
www.evherb.com
17431 East Gale Ave.

City of Industry, CA 91748
(626) 810-5530
(866) 473-3697 (GREEN97)

Heel
www.heelusa.com
10421 Research Road SE
Albuquerque, NM 87192-0280
(800) 621-7644
(505) 293-3843

Pet's Best Pet Health Insurance
www.petsbest.com
*I'm a big fan of pet health insurance in order to reduce the cost
of care. Pet's Best is one of my favorite companies, and they have
agreed to give readers a 5 percent discount on the cost of pet health
insurance, which you can receive when you go to the above link.*

2710 Sunrise Rim Road
Boise, ID 83705
(877) 738-7237

Pet-Togethers
www.pettogethers.com
20701 North Scottsdale Road
Suite 107
Scottsdale, AZ 85255
(480) 282-8520

Bibliography

Messonnier, Shawn. *8 Weeks to a Healthy Dog*. Emmaus, Pennsylvania: Rodale, 2003.

———. *The Allergy Solution for Dogs: Natural and Conventional Therapies to Ease Discomfort and Enhance Your Dog's Quality of Life*. Roseville, California: Prima Publishing, 2000.

———. *The Arthritis Solution for Dogs: Natural and Conventional Therapies to Ease Pain and Enhance Your Dog's Quality of Life*. Roseville, California: Prima Publishing, 2000.

———. *Natural Health Bible for Dogs & Cats: Your A-Z Guide to Over 200 Conditions, Herbs, Vitamins, and Supplements*. Roseville, California: Prima Publishing, 2001.

———. *The Natural Vet's Guide to Preventing and Treating Cancer in Dogs*. Novato, California: New World Library, 2006.

Index

Index

About the Author

Shawn Messonnier, D.V.M., practices integrative medicine at Paws & Claws Animal Hospital in Plano, Texas. He has written numerous articles on pet care for publications, including *Veterinary Product News, Pet Business, Dog Fancy, Cat Fancy, Cats Magazine, body + soul,* and *Animal Wellness.* Dr. Shawn has authored more than twenty books, including *The Arthritis Solution for Dogs, The Allergy Solution for Dogs,* the award-winning *The Natural Health Bible for Dogs & Cats, 8 Weeks to a Healthy Dog,* and *The Natural Vet's Guide to Preventing and Treating Cancer in Dogs.*

He is a member of several animal and veterinary organizations, including the Association of Avian Veterinarians, the Association of Reptilian and Amphibian Veterinarians, the American Holistic Veterinary Medical Association, Dog Writers Association of America, and Cat Writers' Association.

Dr. Shawn is host of the award-winning *Dr. Shawn, The Natural Vet*, on Martha Stewart Living Radio on Sirius. He currently consults with several pet-care companies including Pet-Togethers. He was voted Best Veterinarian in Dallas, Texas, by *D* magazine.